KINDS OF POWER

KINDS OF POWER

A GUIDE TO ITS INTELLIGENT USES

JAMES HILLMAN

CURRENCY DOUBLEDAY

NEW YORK • LONDON • TORONTO • SYDNEY • AUCKLAND

A CURRENCY BOOK

PUBLISHED BY DOUBLEDAY

a division of Bantam Doubleday Dell Publishing Group, Inc.

1540 Broadway, New York, New York 10036

CURRENCY and DOUBLEDAY are trademarks of Doubleday, a division of
Bantam Doubleday Dell Publishing Group, Inc.

Kinds of Power was originally published by Currency Doubleday in 1995.

DESIGN BY JULIE DUQUET

The Library of Congress has cataloged the hardcover edition as follows:

Hillman, James.

Kinds of power : a guide to its intelligent uses / James Hillman.—1st ed.

p.   cm.

Includes index.

1. Power (Social sciences)

2. Psychology, Industrial.   I. Title.

HM136.H47   1995

303.3—dc20

94-32450

CIP

Neither necessity nor desire, but the love of power, is the demon of mankind. You may give men everything possible—health, food, shelter, enjoyment—but they are and remain unhappy and capricious, for the demon waits and waits; and must be satisfied. Let everything else be taken away from men, and let this demon be satisfied, and then they will nearly be happy—as happy as men and demons can be.

—FRIEDRICH NIETZSCHE,
The Dawn of Day

CONTENTS

KINDS OF POWER

OPENING THE BOOK

This book addresses the psychology of business. As a writer on psychology, I am turning to business for my audience because that is where I believe the most daring and challenged minds are at work and where issues of power are most central. The psychology of business does not belong only to businessmen and businesswomen, to those literally engaged in industry, commerce and economics. For all of us, business provides the main reason to get up in the morning and the organizing principle for each day. To go about your day is to go about your business. Business provides the ideas which shape our lives—their successes, their values, their ambitions. The drama of business, its struggles, challenges, victories and defeats, forms the fundamental myth of our civilization, the story that explains the underlying bottom line of the ceremonies of our behavior. What we live in daily life are the basic ideas of business —earning, spending, saving, producing, appraising, owning, selling. . . . We might like to believe love determines our destiny or that the deep dreams and passions of the soul, or the advances of the technological sciences, are the truly formative factors that direct our lives. In actual living, however, only the ideas of business are always with us, from driveway to desk, from dawn to dusk.

Among the ideas of business, "power" rules the roost. It is the invisible demon that gives rise to our motivations and choices. Power stands behind our fear of loss and desire for control; it seems to offer the ultimate rewards. And so, power will be given the widest space and addressed in a variety of ways in the following chapters.

Power does not appear nakedly as such but wears the disguises of authority, control, prestige, influence, fame, etc. To get to the full nature of power we need to look into and see through its many styles so as to know the unique and specific ways these ideas of power operate in our daily psychology. And though ideas about power provide the overt content of the following pages, the power of ideas is the latent content of the book as a whole. For as you and I muse and mull, we are both all the while engaged—not with a thing or a fact called "power," but with *ideas*. This introduction will try to press home why I think this distinction is so utterly crucial.

The calendar on the wall, ominous in its power, declares to all alike that we are living during the conclusion of a century, of a millennium, of an aeon, and the journals of science report a vast extinction of biological forms comparable to the Ice Age. Migrations, plagues, rapacious destruction, toxicity; geographical, genetic and biochemical alterations profoundly shake faith in the progress of historical continuity. Old hopes are in disarray; the future is uncertain—the very ideas of "past" and "future" decon-struct, for we can no longer tell predictions from fantasies or records and memories from interpretations. What can we go on? What goods are truly durable? The business world, as part of the whole world, feels these tectonic shifts in its soul and seeks to shore up its basic ideas. What ideas can empower business to maintain the powerful posi-tion it still holds over our lives as the pages of the calendar turn?

Ideas of business, such as goods, exchange, cost, mar-ket, demand, profit, property, may have been abstracted originally from the simple arrangements of barter and trade; now these ideas have taken root as independent enti-ties and have grown into an immensely complicated organ-ism called the Economy that embraces the entire world, developed and underdeveloped, free market and managed, industrialized and archaic. The Economy, the God of world civilization, has even been replaced by a takeover merger, nationalism and national security. The multinational cor-poration commands more "power" than many national governments and its power depends on the state of its economy. Business, as defined by the ideas of Western capitalism, has become the fundamental force in human society and, in the manner of any monotheism, promul-gates a fundamentalist faith in its basic tenets. Business has defeated everything in its path. Its last enemies are the oldest: it is still defied by the ancient Gods of blood re-venge, territorial tribalism and the strangely recurrent death struggles between genders, as well as by the untamed divinities of nature—the oceans, the deserts, the magma at the earth's core and the powers of storm and rain. They alone remain to affront and disrupt the power of business. Environmental battles are where the wars of religion are fought today, showing that the old pagan nature Gods have not altogether been subdued by the world unification plans of god, the Economy.

The Economy differs from other world empires, depending neither on Roman legions nor on British battleships, secret police, or stockpiles of nuclear weapons. Its power, like that of religions, has become interiorized. It rules by psychological means. The Economy determines who is included and who marginalized, distributing the rewards and punishments of wealth and poverty, advantage and disadvantage. Because this internalization of its ideas is so unquestioningly and universally accepted, it is the Economy where the contemporary unconscious resides and where psychological analysis is most needed. Our personal lives are no longer the place of unconsciousness—every therapy session, recovery group and family counseling, every afternoon talk show and soap opera have opened wide the closets of private passions and pains. The unconscious is exactly what the word says: what is least conscious because it is most usual, most familiar, most everyday. That is the daily round of business.

Because of its world rule, the ideas of business, especially the idea which sustains its power—the idea of power itself—must become a focus for any psychology that would try to understand the members of contemporary society. Business is not merely a factor, one component among many affecting our lives. Its ideas provide the basic inescapable warp and woof on which the patterns of our behaviors are woven. We can't get away from the Economy. To set aside the profit motive, the desire to possess, the ideals of fair wage and economic justice, the bitterness over taxation, the fantasies of inflation and depression, the appeal of saving, to ignore the psychopathologies of dealing, collecting, consuming, selling and working, and yet pretend to grasp the interior life of persons in our society would be like analyzing the peasants, craftsmen, ladies and nobles of medieval society all the while ignoring Christian theology, as if it were merely an inconsequential occurrence. Economics is our contemporary theology, regardless of how we spend Sunday. Economics is the only effective syncretistic cult remaining in the world today, our world's only ecumenical faith. It provides the daily ritual, uniting Christian, Hindu, Mormon, atheist, Buddhist, Sikh, Adventist, animist, evangelist, Muslim, Jew, fundamentalist and New-Ager in the common temple, admitting all alike, from which the money changers have not been thrown out, the Swiss bank.

Nothing shows more vividly the power of business than the anxieties in both Hong Kong and the People's Republic of China over their agreed unification. Whereas the fears of Hong Kong take rise in the old geopolitical imagination—a tiny harbor enclave swallowed up by a giant continental nation with its billion people—the fears of Beijing recognize the immense power of the ideas of business, represented by Hong Kong, which can forever alter the political philosophy and conduct of life of those very same billions.

Since business exercises such dominion over each of us, we must know how its power operates. What is its nature? What constitutes the power of business, enabling it to have such sway? Business has no standing army, no ruling king who must be obeyed, no SWAT teams or secret police, no codified laws or educational dogma for indoctrinating youth, no concerted political program or national party, no church, credo, priests or holy writ. Wherein lies its power?

The answer can be found only in the pervasiveness of its ideas. Our contemporary civilization is held together neither by ideas of beauty, truth, justice, or fate, nor by military force like the *pax romana,* nor by common laws, divinities, language or shared beliefs. Only the ideas of business are actually universal. If the ideas of business, such as trade, property, product, exchange, value, profit, money, are the ideas that consciously and unconsciously rule the planet's human life, then these are the ideas that conjoin to give business its power, establishing its world empire across all borders of geography and barriers of custom. These ideas trickle down into each act of making, serving, choosing, and keeping that we perform. We are

each, every one of us, in business. We now have one answer to what constitutes the power of business?

But this answer leaves an even larger question begging:
What is power? Examining that immense question (equal
to what is nature, beauty, soul, truth, love, life, or human
being) will be the occupation of this book.

So this book's main task is to examine a multitude of
major ideas that are carried by the term "power." Not an
easy task, in view of a general hesitancy to study power
straight on. Physics prefers the words "energy" and
"force"; logic speaks rather of "cause" and "necessity,"
and psychology, of "dynamics." Where ideas of power do
appear, however, they are in the fields of politics and religion, those two areas that are notoriously disruptive to
calm conversation because of the fury they can release.
Since politics and religion are where we find ideas of power
prevalent in discussion and fundamental to that discussion,
this book will draw examples from politics and parallels
with religion. In other parts of this book I shall also draw
upon the language of people not involved with politics or
religion, how they imagine power, hold power, use power,
long for it and fear it. All this exposure should shower
upon the mind of business the seeds of new thoughts for its
activities. In addition, this book will turn to business itself
for ideas tangential to its power such as the ideas of
"growth" and "efficiency," and finally for myths that unconsciously underlie attitudes and practices in business.

This book intends to affect the minds of its readers in three ways. *First,* it wants to disturb sedimented habits of thinking about power, especially easy ideas that make us believe we know what it is and can have it in our hands, easy ideas like: "Money is power," or Francis Bacon's dictum, "Knowledge is power," which has now become "Information is power," a maxim that seemed to keep J. Edgar Hoover at the helm of the FBI for years after the myth of the honest G-man had been torn to tatters by the winds of change. Other easy ideas insist power is force: "Political power grows out of the barrel of a gun" (Mao Zedong) and "Guns will make us powerful; butter will only make us fat" (Hermann Göring). Then there are the familiar statements like "Power is measurable by the rate of work done," and "Power corrupts," and warnings like "A friend in power is a friend lost" (Henry Adams), or these two generalities from Emerson: "Life is a search after power . . ." and "All power is of one kind, a sharing of the nature of the world." Another widespread conventional wisdom is that one can learn power at a business school, from a self-help guide or by interning with a top-gun executive. Too easy. Too simple.

In contrast with the simple notions are the difficult definitions proposed by philosophers, for instance: "Power is the compulsion of composition" (A. N. Whitehead); "[Power is] the production of intended effects" (B. Russell); "[Power is] the difference in probability of an event, given certain actions by A, and the probability of the event given no such actions by A" (R. A. Dahl); "Inherent in power, therefore, as opposed to force, is a certain extension in space and time" (E. Canetti); "By virtue and power I mean the same thing; that is, virtue, insofar as it is referred to man, is a man's nature or essence" (Spinoza).

After these mind-bending clarifications, we long again for the first aid of simple explanations. But as Einstein said: "Everything should be as simple as it can be, but not simpler." The seduction of simplicity tempts ever more as issues become more and more complex, so that voices of simplicity, like Reagan and Perot, offer mental peace without mental effort. Simple ideas feel comfortable; they don't give trouble. They seem to let issues settle down quietly into the bottom mud of the mind, all tension and sophistication denied. A simple idea of power, any idea that defines it simply, lulls us into quiescent passivity, and so actually saps power. The mind needs richer foods and it likes to move subtly, like a snake or a fox, otherwise it will get blindsided by the narrowness of focus, thereby blocking access to power and the enjoyment of it. If we don't first disturb the mind's familiar concepts of power, we can hardly be smart when using it. If, for instance, I define power simply as "control," I will never be able to let go of control without fear of losing power. Trapped by this concept into paranoid vigilance, competitive exertions and demonstrative leadership, I will never discover the subtle power of influence, authority, generosity or patient resistance. Ideas need to be shaken before they can clarify. So I am inviting disturbance.

To think through an idea it helps to study its appearances. Power pops up all over the place; power brokers and power lunches; power books and power surges; power steering and power tools; power trips and power freaks; even power songs and power animals of New Age shamanism. The general idea, power, calls for differentiation, and that is the *second* intention of this book: to differentiate the bundles of ideas that compose the word "power" and constitute its baggage. For example, if you should say you "want more power," are you asking for more vital energy, or for more opportunity to dominate messy situations, or for more recognition, or for more tough endurance to bear your burdens? Do you want a more prestigious office and title or to have more authoritative input in decisions. Do you want to lead or to command? Do you want to be loved for your support or respected for your fearsomeness? All these ideas enter into a differentiation of power. In philosophy, the differentiation of a phenomenon by letting it display itself without prejudice—without moralizing, advising, or pressing one position over others—is called the phenomenological method. So this book sets forth a phenomenology of the ideas of power.

The differentiation of styles and varieties leads to a general extension of personal power. That is the *third* intention of this book: to extend the idea of power into regions of feeling, intellect and spirit that reach beyond the exercise of power by the human will. This extension into aspects of power not usually considered in the study of it aims to offer more potential to readers of this book. For this book does intend to be "empowering"—why make the effort of reading it? Empowerment comes from widening your understanding of the kinds of power going on around you and from uncovering a wider spectrum of possibilities for embracing power. You learn these things by the simple means of unwrapping the unconsciousness surrounding the idea of power, rather than by instructions and exercises for practice. Expanding ideas comes first; widened practice follows.

For instance, if the idea of food means only meat and potatoes, my actual diet will be severely restricted. Once the idea of food differentiates, the practice of my eating extends not only into fruit, eggs and cheese, for instance, but into my capacity for eating in ethnic restaurants, traveling in foreign places and sharpening my senses in general.

So, when you finish the book, your idea of power should be disturbed, differentiated and extended.

The way I shall be working the theme is how a psychoanalyst would, for, after all, that is what I am: a longtime teacher and practitioner of psychoanalysis. As in a psychoanalysis, we shall be trying to understand what is intended in our words as we strive for insights that clarify (as well as disturb, differentiate and extend). As in a psychoanalysis, sitting in two chairs, you reading and I writ-

ing, we are engaged with words and the habitual unconscious ideas and feelings they express. While we converse,
other unexpected ideas and feelings rise in our minds,
moving our furniture, and we gain insights and recogni-
tions that will bear on our actions in new and unexpected
ways after we set down the book and the session is over.

Clarification of the mind by attending to language is a
method that begins with Confucius and with Socrates. Both
held that the rectification of any problem begins with the
careful consideration of our speech. Freud continued this
approach. He first called his psychoanalysis "the talking
cure." To become conscious of anything we have first to
get the words right, because words are loaded with implications. You and I may sit across from each other, as in a
therapy session or a business lunch, using the very same
word, like "power," yet we may each be tapping into
radically different ideas buried in the word.

Without attention to words we are dumb—speechless and stupid both. This dumbness (and I do not mean
actual larynx impairment) translates into the blunt and
crude wieldings of power called police brutality, drive-by
shootings, rapes, domestic violence, gratuitous assault, excessive force, drunken speeding, shouting matches, ampli-
fied sound, rude callous manners and small children with
big guns. Language can express every shade of emotion,
that is precisely its beauty—and its power. Deprived of the
sense of words our emotional expressions become primitive, physical and senseless.

The Chinese have said for centuries that people resort to physical violence because their words have failed. Maybe the cure for American violence begins in a talking cure, a cure that begins with attending to the potency of words.

Speechlessness and stupidity appear not only at the violent end of the dumbness spectrum. At the other end we find that hapless dejected disempowerment felt by so many in our nation who cannot find the words for their aimless despair, beyond vague mumblings about "empowerment." Empowerment has become the major catchword for barking people into the self-help and recovery booths at the therapeutic carnival. So many people today feel "disempowered." What is it they, and we, are asking for? Where and why has the power gone that once filled the dream of better times in a better land? Is psychology the place to go to be reempowered? Can individual citizens together with their support groups in sessions taking place all over the country by the hundreds of thousands every evening of the week "find the power"? Before all else we have a job to do with the very idea of power.

As a therapist, I am convinced that the recovery of a sense of power in American society requires more than personal empowerment therapy. Something profound is affecting the contemporary spirit of the society as a whole. It has to do perhaps with the turning pages of the calendar, with the extinctions and pollutions, with retribution exacted by the pagan powers in the soul of the world, reaching the individual's psyche as his and her personal malaise.

But the sensitizing of feeling, of body, and the improvement of communication skills in personal relationships by means of therapy leaves the core of the malaise unaddressed.

This core is collective, and only secondarily individual. That is, the feelings of failure, impotence and entrapment which assail an individual person may well be reflections in the individual of agonies in the collective soul. Ancient thought could not even conceive of the individual's soul life apart from the soul of the world. The core of our personal malaise has a spiritual dimension, not only a psychological one, so psychological attempts at recovery are always only halfway measures. Furthermore, the contemporary malaise afflicting the body politic—or the soul of the nation—is also ideational. Dysfunctional ideas require a therapy too, and not only for the bearers and victims of these ideas. Nor can we expect that skimpy and cheap ideas will be treated by a therapy of emotions. You cannot leave out the head or its left brain and expect critical discernment of media distortions and intelligent improvement in our national debates. No matter how sincerely I work through my feelings in regard to power, if my mind is still entranced by wishful fantasies of growth and efficiency or by simplistic ideas of control, authority, leadership and prestige, I will remain thwarted in my daily struggles with the operations of power in the actual world. Therapy must shake and move the ideas and myths that govern my mind. Otherwise, my well-adapted emotional body with raised self-esteem in its field of positive human relations may well be able to communicate better, jog longer and hold on to a job, yet all the while privately pine for empowerment because I am still unaware of the full complexities of power, and therefore unable to express what is truly desired.

Our problems are inside our lives, yes; but our lives are lived inside fields of power, under the influence of others, in accord with authority, subject to tyrannies. Moreover, our lives are lived inside the fields of power that are our cities with their offices and cars, systems of work and mountains of trash. These too are powers impinging on our souls. When the wider world breaks down and is sick at heart, the individual suffers accordingly. Since he and she are not the underlying cause of their suffering, neither can they be its cure. The collective power failures in government bureaucracies, education, institutions and corporations, the ineffective transmission of power downward to the disenfranchised, oppressed and impoverished, and the sputtering generators of acrid heat below the streets of America's cities require attention to the transformers and dynamos beyond the personal fuse box in your basement. Attention has to be paid to the overhead power lines, those mainline ideas that are the archetypal wirings which energize each of our individualities. Personal recovery cannot substitute for national recovery. At best, they go hand in hand. Dysfunctional ideas in the world of the present, rather than the wounds of the inner child of the past, claim our psychological care today. To recover personal power we must first look at its source in the collective notions of power.

To go to the source, especially in America, calls for a new heartfelt appreciation of ideas in and for themselves. Perhaps ideas are the single most precious miracle in human existence. For ideas determine our goals of action, our styles of art, our values of character, our religious practices and even our ways of loving. It is to this precious power of ideas that this book is dedicated.

The struggle now and always is with the autonomy of ideas, their ability to invade the human mind, seize it and shape its formation into ideologies. Do we really know what has moved into our minds—those ideas, like furniture, that stand silently in the same place for decades determining every move we make in the interior habits of our thoughts and actions. Ideas we have, and do not know we have, have us.

For example, the idea of power as force has captured the American imagination in personal relations, in corporate management and in foreign affairs. This simple equation, Power = Force, has immeasurable consequences all through our culture from the exorbitant cost of the military budget to maintain the United States as a world power, to wife beatings and rape to affirm masculine power, to packing a weapon to assert the power of personal liberty. When, however, power is defined more as influence (connections, nepotism, networking) as in ruling groups in Italy and Japan, or defined by appointment to

and holding on to office as in the old Hapsburg empire of
Austria, then the role of force in society is mitigated by
other styles of power. So, too, in traditional British society
where power was defined more by subordination within an
oppressive class system. London "bobbies" (police) then
carried no weapons: accents and manners were the force
that managed disorderly conduct and kept British subjects
"in their place." Again, when power takes its definition
from relations with ancestors, spirits and powers beyond
the human, then elaborate initiations and taboos alter the
very meaning of force and control indiscriminate violence.
Before our society can practically limit armament spending, protect citizens in the homes and streets or pass effective gun laws we must first become clearer about our notions of power.

The craving for new ideas and for intellectual skills to
deal with the constraining effects of unthought ideas is a
deep hunger in the American soul. This I have found in my
itinerant teaching, private consultations and retreats with
men throughout the country. Relationships may comfort,
support groups nourish and success enhance, but ideas empower the spirit and open its eyes to envisioning possibilities. I do not want to believe that we are essentially a
people obsessed with security (safety, insurance, prisons,
protection, labeling laws); nor that we are a people en-
slaved to consumerism; enchanted by the media, entertainment and celebrity; dependent on relationships; or that we
are a narcissistic society in love with its own childhood to

the utter denial of our national tragedies, unable to imagine a meaningful future. These diagnoses observe symptoms only, without getting to the fundamental syndrome of which the symptoms are but fluctuating and fashionable manifestations. The deeper syndrome is inertia of the spirit, a passivity that feels no vocation and shies from imaginative vision, adventurous thinking and intellectual clarification. That we imagine ourselves today as a nation of victims attests to a vacuum in the spirit of the nation. These are symptoms of the soul in search of clarity. Clarity is the essential.

The soul is desperately seeking the power of mind to be applied to the powerlessness it experiences. Though we want ideas, we haven't learned how to handle them. We use them up too quickly. We get rid of them by immediately putting them into practice. We seem to know only one thing to do with an idea; apply it; convert it into something usable. A "good idea" is good because it saves time or money or makes things more convenient. The idea dies right there in the conversion. It loses its life-generating force. The Greek Stoics spoke of a *logos spermatikos,* the generating word or seminal thought. As these seed ideas are put into practice and concretized, they no longer generate further ideas in the realm of ideas.

When Dr. Joycelyn Elders opens the idea of legalizing currently illegal drugs or when the Libertarians suggest elimination of the personal income tax, we rush to judgment, at once arguing the practical or impractical implications of these ideas. Whom would they benefit and whom would they harm; what would they cost; how would their practice be managed; what would the effect be on the budget, the welfare system, health care, the inner city, the defense projections? The debate focuses on hypothetical "facts," models of implementation and the morals of opinions and positions, all the while neglecting the further shores of thought and feeling. For the ideas prompted by the seeds sown by Dr. Elders or the Libertarians foster ramifications in the realm of thought quite apart from the how-tos of practice. Legalized drugs invite ideas of youth, addiction, pharmaceuticals, alcohol, freedom, cities, pleasures, while taxes conjure up the complex problems of political science—the nature of government, the relation of earning to spending and the principles of taxation as tithing, as charity, as penalty, as communal sharing and so forth. Fixed upon the "how" and the "who," we avoid playing with the "what," turning it over in our mind, an idea as an entertainment, ideation as a sport that gives as much fun and mental exercise as do many other kinds of play. Unfortunately, we are not a nation that talks ideas late into the night because we are tired from having struggled to put them into practice.

Therefore, in what follows I shall not be elaborating direct applications for business organizations and their managerial conundrums. I worry lest the birds be caged too soon. First, let's think about what comes into the mind, get the feel of it, asking that it be pondered, weighed. Nor shall slow patient reasoning or the amassing of evidence be the method in the following pages. My idea about ideas is that they first need to be *entertained*. Then they may spark better ones in your mind and can lead to unforeseeable implementation in your life. My tactic is more to explode than to explain, more to keep the ideas brief, quick, heated and scattered, in whatever way I can— polemical excess, farfetched fantasy or passionate assault on conventions we hold dear. Take what follows as detection, brainstorming, improvisation, free-style drawing of things unseen. Please, we're not in a classroom and I am not your instructor. Let's talk ideas.

Since ideas are our quarry, it makes sense to get clearer about what they are. The Greek word for "idea," *eidos,* comes from *idein,* "to see," and is related to the noun, which means two things: (a) something seen like a form and (b) a way of seeing like a perspective. We both see ideas and see by means of them. They are both the forms our minds take and what allows our minds to form events into shaped experiences.

The first classic sense of idea as *a visible appearance* like a sharply defined mental or verbal image arose in the modern age with Descartes (1596–1650) when he searched for "clear and distinct ideas" on which to base his entire philosophy and our Western way of thinking ever since. Such is the power of an idea! For Platonic metaphysicians, ideas exist in a supersensible reality accessible only to reason, imagination and memory—and perhaps magical practices. They would claim you can think ideas, imagine them and remember them—and perhaps manipulate them (mind control, propaganda, indoctrination). But you cannot touch or feel them.

Ideas come into our minds. We "get" an idea, and can be "taken" by an idea. Their mode of arrival may be via flashes of inspiration, long mullings and musings, dreams or hard concentrated attention. They often move from mind to mind, the property of no one. Sometimes the same idea can occur in different places and different minds at the same time. That ideas can persuade us, even convert us, gives them immense power like a revelatory vision, as in the visions of John in the fourth Gospel, where *eidos* is something visibly perceived just as a spirit voice is audibly heard. The "coming in" of an idea that leads to a discovery is expressed by the Latin word *invenire,* from which comes our word "invention." All our inventions begin as ideas; all our material power derives from ideational power.

The second classic sense of idea as *a way of seeing,* a perspective, means that ideas open your eyes. Fresh ideas are new ways of seeing. Phrases like "Do you see what I mean?" and "See what I'm saying" and "Look at it this way" combine both senses of idea: idea as entity and as perspective.

Since ideas are already operating in our perspectives, as for instance when we say, "That's your perception; my idea is different," turning ideas over and looking at them carefully becomes paramount for every endeavor of any kind. Because we take our usual ideas for granted, ideas (as supersensible powers) have us in their grip without our realizing it. That's why the investigation of them is freeing and the encouraging of ideas is enriching. One idea in particular blocks the examination of ideas from the start: the belief that we make them up in our own heads, as if secreted from the human brain. We attempt to disguise their autonomous power by attaching human names to technical inventions, physical discoveries, medical procedures and mathematical laws, thereby attributing ideas to the practical persons who supposedly thought them up. The poet W. H. Auden saw through this humanistic delusion that tries to harness their freedom, saying, "We are lived by powers we pretend to understand."

"Practical men," supposedly said John Maynard Keynes, this century's most influential economist, "are usually slaves of some defunct economist." Implication: ideas need liberation; they need to be born again else they become not merely defunct but delusional. One such delusional idea, showing more and more its rigor mortis yet still adhered to by practical men, is that of the bottom line. Holistic accounting as well as everyday evidence shows that clean-up costs, depletion of resources, litigation, property protection, i.e., all the societal side effects of private-sector profit become the burden of the public sector. What the corporation does not compute into its costs will be paid for by the public, or added to its debt. Someone must pick up the tab. And so higher taxes follow inevitably from higher profitability. Taxes are some of the tribute exacted from the slaves devoted to a defunct economic idea, the bottom line.

If our civilization is to continue, it will require vital ideas such as the astonishing plethora articulated by the Founding Fathers at the end of the eighteenth century. For ideas to be born and stay alive through their precarious infancy they must be welcomed warmly so that their native power can come fully to mind. Skepticism and irony don't belong at the start. At first, better the wacky and the weird than ideas whittled down to fit preconceived slots. Here we need courage to face their destructive force, for ideas also can lay waste cherished habits of mind. We now call this destruction of old ideas, politely, a "paradigm shift." "Catastrophe theory" would be more appropriate. The vitality of a culture depends less on its hopes and its history than on its capacity to entertain willingly the divine and daimonic force of ideas.

1

THE CHANGING
HEROICS OF POWER

INTRODUCTION

Much of the basic furniture standing around in our minds was set there by Victorians between the 1830s and 1890s. It belongs to the heroic age of industrialism and imperialism, deriving its style from steam engines and railroad tracks extending into a limitless horizon, from cheap electricity that illumines dark places at the flick of a switch and cheap labor that works at the flick of another switch, from established class hierarchy, competitive victories, mega-monopolies, from conquests of every sort—over diseases, geographical obstacles, indigenous peoples and the soul's irrationalities. Our minds are still furnished with oak armoires stuffed with heroic uniforms and portraits of tough-jawed patriots, the great inventors and engineers, generals and colonizers, composers and novelists, all of heroic proportions and accomplishments.

Indigenous peoples of the Pacific Northwest coast carved giant totem poles of their ancestor spirits, providing icons of power for the tribe. Business too has heroic ghosts continuing to live in its ideas and ancestral figures on which it relies for inspiration and whom it emulates in ambition, for these giants could turn things around and get things done. They changed the world, much as the legendary heroes like Hercules, who diverted whole rivers to clean up old messes; like Marduk, who drained the sucking swamps; like Moses, who freed his people and drowned their pursuers. These are take-charge figures of command and control. Whatever stands in the way can be met by fixing or fighting.

Power has been defined for us by our inheritance. The statuary in our parks, the stories in our schoolbooks, the program notes at the concert reinforce heroic accomplishment against odds by effort of will. Power is persuasive force, muscular struggle, decisive command, productive result, widest practical usefulness. Power is imaged by the winner, even the slayer.

These inherited furnishings are not easy to move, especially since they are remnants of social Darwinism, the philosophical base of the modern age. Social Darwinism can be condensed into a sequence of propositions. Progress is natural. What is natural is God-given. Therefore, progress is good. Progress advances by means of natural selection; the superior rise and the inferior fall out. There are always more at the bottom than at the top, more weeds than hybrid roses, so hierarchy is natural. Because of the numerically narrowing ascending pyramid, natural selection requires competition which allows the fittest to survive. Only the fittest survive the competitive struggle. Survival is assured by getting to the top, and staying on top. (Smaller units of the furnishings that accompany "getting to the top" include: larger market share, increasing return on investment and vertical integration from raw materials to retail sales point.)

Each of these formulas regarding progress, selection, survival and upward struggle can be subsumed under one dominant idea: growth. That word carries a marvelously effective message. Because growth invites images from nature like burgeoning trees and ripening fruit, and the longings of childhood to get bigger and stronger and take charge, the word "growth" delivers the heroic message more effectively than concepts such as "progress," "advancement" or "development." Growth has come to be a major indication of power and a term that substitutes for it, since the ability to grow assumes an innate potential to survive and to win out in the competitive jungle. "Grow or die" stands like a Victorian grandfather clock pressuring our lives twenty-four hours a day.

When we look into the idea of growth we find it tied with a companion equally important, the idea of efficiency. Growth by itself can mean fruitlessly detailed exfoliation, choking weeds, entangled interlocking networks, aimless expansion, redundancy everywhere. Bureaucracy is simply natural growth moved indoors. Because natural growth is extravagantly profligate, growth requires efficiency to keep it functional, to ensure survival. Survival of the fittest translates into survival of the efficient. This translation occurs easily because social Darwinism and its biological metaphors flourished in the same Victorian period as industrialism and its mechanical metaphors such as efficiency. Efficiency, too, just doesn't happen by itself. It depends upon careful measurement, thinking in numbers and decisions based on them. This today we call "cost accounting," "cost-benefit analysis," "cost-effectiveness," "cost-efficient," "bottom line." These are the newer modernist office fittings nailed to the floor of the mind of business and kept in place by specialists called accountants.

Whether the ideas of growth and efficiency are rooted in organic or in mechanical models, both express the old heroics of moving forward against such enemies as inertia, sloth, disorder and confusion, of not sliding backward into the arms of comforting habit and of accomplishing deeds by getting work done. The capacity to get work done is perhaps the simplest definition of power. Hence, the title of this Part, "The Changing Heroics of Power."

But there is a trick in this Part. We will lay out two kinds of heroics, calling them old and new. Growth and efficiency will be balanced out with service and maintenance. From the perspective of the old heroics, service and maintenance seem rearguard actions, cleanup operations, necessary evils. So the task before us requires new ways of thinking about service and maintenance since they occupy a major place in all business planning, in all operations of human life. As long as they are imagined as a dragging impediment, we will not be able to sense just how crucial they have become in the business of business. Service and maintenance challenge the old heroic notions of business to its core.

Today, the heroic challenge forces a confrontation with heroism itself. Heroism is asked to face its own myth, thereby releasing the imagination to find other ways to think about power which has been defined for so long by heroic notions. Heroism, today, rather than focusing on turning problems around, has to turn itself around, inventing new ideas about the old heroics, re-visioning what *today* is pathbreaking and innovative, what *today* are the enemies of accomplishment. It is of little use to open bold new paths if you are still inside the same labyrinth. The model itself must break open.

Perhaps the enemy of heroic action is not where it used to be—the inertia of raw materials, the sloth of labor, the drag of tradition. Perhaps, the enemy that must be overcome lies right at the heart of heroism itself, its own inertia, sloth and resistance in confronting the heroic mode. Until it faces itself it remains in denial, unable to see its own self-destructive propensities even as it redoubles its efforts of heroic action. Because the movement of classic heroism is forward and upward, the most difficult of all tasks for heroic consciousness is looking inward into its own drive, the myth that propels it toward its cruel end: Hercules gone mad; Jesus crucified; Oedipus blind; Agamemnon murdered by his wife; Moses dead, away from the Promised Land. Can giant corporations like GM, IBM and

Kmart and powerful nations like the United States that rose to preeminence by means of dedication to the heroics of expansion and improvement awaken to the tragic consequences of the model that onced served so well? Can heroism shift its own paradigm?

If new styles of heroism are called for, then service and maintenance rise to high value, while growth and efficiency will be imagined altogether differently. Otherwise, the inertia of nineteenth-century modes of thought will direct the hands of twenty-first-century electronics. The machinery may radically change, but unless the mind moves its myths, Hercules, Marduk and Moses still occupy the executive suite. The intelligent exercise of power begins in the mind that has insight into the deeper structures of its actions. Let's look at the first one of these structures that so affect our notions of power: efficiency.

EFFICIENCY

The dictionary's first meaning of power is simply "ability to do or act; capability of accomplishing something," so that much power means, as the dictionary says, "strength," "might." Strong power, power at its starkest, can be defined by two obvious traits: absolute subjugation of conditions and maximum efficiency of operations. In fact, the first depends on the second because power requires efficiency to maintain itself. You cannot stay on top of conditions if your modes of operation are inefficient. Does this further suggest that the purest efficiency will offer the most power?

The extermination camp in German-occupied Poland, Treblinka, and its commandant, Franz Stangl, present efficiency at its purest. Treblinka was the largest of five camps built exclusively for the purpose of extermination. According to a most conservative estimate these camps killed close to 3,000,000 people in seventeen months.

The extermination camps were devised for the Final Solution because an earlier method—simply shooting masses of people above open pits to be bulldozed under (a method used by the Nazis in the Soviet Union)—was soon rejected as inefficient for what Himmler was to call "the enormous task ahead."* This method was inefficient for many reasons: the escaping gases from corpse putrefaction gave an indication of what was happening; no salvage of goods and gold; open-pit killing took too many soldiers to do the shooting, so that secrecy could not be maintained; too much confusion, some victims mimicked death, some escaped, some soldiers did not shoot, etc. Efficiency here is to be understood solely from the viewpoint of the one in power, the executor. An efficient execution in other situations takes the victim's viewpoint: quick, painless, neither cruel nor unusual.

Here is an excerpt from one of the seventy interviews conducted by Gitta Sereny with Franz Stangl (pp. 169–70):

"How many people would arrive on a transport?" I asked Stangl.

"Usually about five thousand. Sometimes more."

"Did you ever talk to any of the people who arrived?"

"Talk? No . . . usually I'd be working in my office—there was a great deal of paperwork—till about eleven. Then I made my next round, starting up at the *Totenlager*. By that time they were well ahead with the work up there." (He meant that by this time the 5,000 to 6,000 people who had arrived that morning were dead: the "work" was the disposal of the bodies, which took most of the rest of the day and frequently contin-

---

* Gitta Sereny, *Into That Darkness* (New York: Random House/Vintage, 1983), p. 98. (Subsequent references to this book are by page numbers.)

ued during the night.) "Oh, by that time of the morning everything was pretty much finished in the lower camp. A transport was normally dealt with in two or three hours. At twelve I had lunch. . . . Then another round and more work in the office."

My aim here is not to psychoanalyze Stangl, his motives, his conscience or the societal, political and religious support on which he could rely for his "work." Nor will I philosophize about European history, the theology of the Holocaust, the nature of evil, or upon systematic routine and schedule as independent archetypal forces. I am here restricting our attention to the idea of efficiency.

Furthermore, I am asking you to read these passages as examples of managerial thinking in the face of overwhelmingly difficult conditions. Treblinka as a system was a large-scale industrial complex, and Stangl was its chief executive officer, on whose shoulders responsibility lay. Failure for him was worse than failure; it was death. The person called Stangl is the shadow figure looming behind Everyman at an office desk.

The "work" of gassing and burning five thousand human beings in a morning or anywhere from five to twenty thousand persons (p. 197) in twenty-four hours requires the maximum efficiency: no wasted motions, no friction, no complications, no backlog. "They arrived, and they were dead within two hours," Stangl said (p. 199).

In order to get at all close to how efficient the camp's operations were, we have first to imagine the potential for chaotic disorder harnessed by its efficiency. The trains came into the camp on a one-track line. They had to be unloaded (the already dead on arrival dumped into a pit) and shunted out, keeping the track clear for the next train. Men, women and children, all ages, staggered out of the cars, blinded by daylight or floodlight, terrorized and confused, half dead from suffocation, dehydrated, dazed, feeble, hysterical, not understanding the commands. If they turned left instead of right, faltered, missed an order, hesitated, raised a question, they delayed the procedure and were often whipped forward or promptly shot on the spot. Nothing must interfere with the efficiency of the procedures.

"Could you not have changed that?" I asked. "In your position, could you not have stopped the nakedness, the whips, the horror of the cattle pens?"

"No, no, no. This was the system. Wirth had invented it. It worked. And because it worked it was irreversible."

But the "work" was not over with death. The camp had to be maintained, the ovens kept in repair, the supplies of fuel and lethal gas replenished, the staff managed, secrecy kept, and also the valuables inventoried, the clothes, the gold, the piles of human hair, and as Stangl says, the paperwork. And "it worked." The absolute rule of efficiency.

The first clear articulation of efficiency in Western thought occurs neither in the mechanics of physics nor in theories of economic productivity, but in Aristotle's *Physics* and *Metaphysics*. Aristotle divided the answer to the question "why?" into four kinds of causes: *formal,* the idea or archetypal principle that governs an event; *final,* the purpose, or that for the sake of which the event is intended; *material,* the substance that is worked upon and changed; and *efficient,* that which initiates a motion and is the immediate instigator of change.

The classic example is that of a statue. A sculptor (efficient cause) produces changes in a block of marble (material cause), for the purpose of a beautiful object (final cause), with the idea of a statue in mind (formal cause). All four causes are necessary; none can be excluded. The idea of a book (formal cause) and of this book in particular is as important as the efficient writing of it, the material paper, ink, glue and binding that compose its volume, and the intent to communicate ideas (final cause).

As philosophers shifted their interests through the centuries, the efficient cause took on an ever greater role. Moralists claimed the final cause for ethics and theology while the material cause fell to the scientific analysis of the physics of matter and motion. The formal cause—so important to the classical philosophers following Aristotle—dwindled into arbitrary definitions and descriptions without any effective power.

By the time of John Locke in the seventeenth century, whose notions of individual freedom are fundamental to American political life, the efficient cause became the sole answer to the question "why?" The chapter on power in his *Essay Concerning Human Understanding* derives the idea of power from the human will—that it can begin, direct and stop actions. The efficient cause as power explains why things happen; it governs all events. Freedom is power unfettered; the will unconstrained. The efficient cause merges with the idea of power itself and even becomes a kind of substance, the basic real force which moves the world as the will moves the body.

The efficient cause makes things happen. When it is singled out as the *only* cause, then it does not matter what happens, to what or whom it happens and for what purpose it happens. Stangl's gross fault—philosophically—lies in a one-sided dedication to the efficient cause without seeing, or feeling, the other three. When the efficient cause becomes stripped of its correlative partners, it can lose all touch with the actualities of life. The facts that the materials worked on are human beings, that the essential nature of the action is murder and that the final goal is death are all subordinated in value or lost to awareness altogether, owing to the intense focus on the procedures of efficiency. In contemporary psychological language, *efficiency is a primary mode of denial*. Stangl makes this clear in his explanations. His single-minded devotion to doing an efficient job closed his eyes to what the job was actually doing. His efficiency defended him from his sensitivity. Work justified itself; efficiency for its own sake—and it could not be stopped "because it worked."

Some twenty years ago Richard Nixon used the justification of efficiency in denying the profound and complex implications of Watergate. His basic defense for his prolonged cover-up (denial) rested upon the overriding importance of doing the job of running the government and leading the nation toward world peace, justice and security; all the while the very cover-up was sapping the government's capacity to lead and to govern. In another instance Nixon ordered the heavy bombing of North Vietnam as the efficient means to end the war. The decision based on efficiency seemed to take little account of the other causes: the essential nature of the violence, its long-term ends for all those involved and the material cost.

Two insanely dangerous consequences result from raising efficiency to the level of an independent principle. First, it favors short-term thinking—no looking ahead, down the line; and it produces insensitive feeling—no looking around at the life values being lived so efficiently. Second, means become ends; that is, doing something becomes the full justification of doing regardless of what you do. Operational phrases in business life such as "just do it," "get it done," "don't ask questions," "not excuses, results!" are telltale signs of the efficiency principle beginning to separate from its cohorts and set off on its own.

The ethical confusions now plaguing business, government and the professions, although having many varied sources, result in part from the pressures of efficiency as a value in and for itself. Then, curiously, Aristotle's other principles seem to return from repressive exclusion only to sabotage efficiency. Inefficiency becomes a favorite mode of rebellion against the tyranny of efficiency: slowdown, work-to-rule, buck-passing, absenteeism, delayed responses, mislaid documents, unreturned phone calls. Ethical protest against the tyranny of efficiency employ these modes of inefficiency. It is as if in the name of being a good citizen with concern for the wider implications of a job, one must become a "bad" worker.

I am arguing here that the idea of efficiency per se does not provide sufficient reason for human action. It must always be attached to its partners, the other three causes, and serve within a complex tension of reasons. It is not enough to like doing a job, to perform it well or to do a job because it must be done and it provides you security. Stangl could claim to some degree all these reasons. Besides these justifications in defense of your actions, which attempt to answer the question "why?" (why do you do what you are doing?), attention must be paid to the basic causes. What are the material effects of your efficiency? What are you doing to the material nature of the world? What is the essence of what you are doing; what formal principle governs it? And, above all, what is its purpose, or in Aristotle's phrase, "that for the sake of which" your efficient actions are performed?

Gitta Sereny pressed Stangl for the final cause (that for the sake of which the "work" at Treblinka was carried out). In their many talks, he mentioned fear, survival and the uselessness of protest. Finally, she asked him (p. 232):

"What did you think at the time was the reason for the exterminations?" His answer came at once: "They wanted the Jews' money."

"You can't be serious?"

He was bewildered by my reaction of disbelief. "But of course. Have you any idea of the fantastic sums that were involved? That's how the steel in Sweden was bought."

Stangl's final cause, his nuts-and-bolts purpose for the exterminations he so efficiently supervised, was to get "the Jews' money." It was not racism and the extermination of undesirables. It was not nationalism and the betterment of the German people. It was not hatred, fear, revenge. It was not loyalty to a leader or a cause, or for the sake of a better future. Stangl's final cause was devoid of all ideals and passions; no other end but profit.

No other end but profit—Nietzsche had an insight into this combination of profit, power, fanatical efficiency and criminality in 1881 *(The Dawn of Day)*:

Whence arises this excessive impatience in our day which turns men into criminals? . . . three-fourths of our upper classes indulge in legalized fraud, and suffer from the pangs of conscience that follow dealings on the stock exchange: What gives rise to all this? It is not real want . . . but they are

urged on day and night by a terrible impatience . . . and by
an equally terrible longing and love for gold. In this impa-
tience and love, however, we see reappear once more the desire
for power which was stimulated in former times by the belief
that we were in the possession of truth, a fanaticism which bore
such beautiful names that we could dare to be inhuman with a
good conscience (burning Jews, heretics, and good books, and
exterminating entire cultures superior to ours, such as those of
Peru and Mexico). The means of this desire for power are
changed in our day, but the same volcano is still smoldering,
impatience and intemperate love call for their victims, and what
was once done "for the love of God" is now done for the love of
money; i.e., for the love of that which at present affords us the
highest feeling of power and a good conscience.

Today, the preeminence of profit is called bottom-line thinking, obeisance to the god Economics. The final cause has become the bottom line, which provides the philosophical ground for the heightened purism of efficiency (possibly another name for fascism?) at the expense of the other two causes, material and formal. Materials may be exploited, whether raw stuffs or laboring hands, and the formal—that is, aesthetic and ethical—considerations may be ignored both in the acts of production and in the goods produced and sold. Efficiency for the sake of the bottom line rules.

Anyone who justifies decisions by referring to the bottom line has something to learn from Treblinka. Cost-efficiency needs some honest reflection. If cost-efficiency compares with its analog in physics—output equals input less friction—then the most efficient, or profitable, system eliminates the most friction; move fast through the "tube" into the gas chamber. Stangl, too, had to give the most bang for the buck. Because every exchange is always a relationship, to get the most while giving the least is unjust, unethical, antisocial, abusive, perhaps "evil." Yet predatory commerce ("the free market" as it is euphemistically called) operates regularly on the principle of "get the most and pay the least." Predatory commerce differs from Treblinka only in degree, not in principle.

There are businesses today dedicated to "the double bottom line"—profit *and* social responsibility. These companies are attempting to yoke the motive of profit together with the other motivations. They are harnessing efficiency with concern for nature (material cause), aesthetic values (formal cause) and spiritual principles (final cause). They still seek efficiency (profit) but not at the cost of the well-being of their employees, the communities where the business is located, the implications for the wider world. The double bottom line protects against efficiency as an autonomous and isolated cause just as it recognizes that a company is not an autonomous power isolated within its property lines.

It is well to keep in mind the image of Treblinka when we ask government to be more "efficient." To expect the post office, the passenger railroads, the interstate highways, the prison system or the national parks to show a profit forgets that government is fundamentally a service industry as stated in the Constitution. Its efficiency can be judged only in terms of the services it provides—that they meet the needs of the people who grant its power. For a candidate for political office to campaign on a platform of efficiency in government suggests the infiltration of fascistic ideals. Mussolini made the trains run on time—but at what cost?

The extermination camps belong continually in our Western consciousness, not only to remind us of the human capacity for atrocity, the pathological potential in systematic technology, the virulence of racism, the existence of evil or the death of both the Jewish and Christian God. The camps belong continually in consciousness because the devotion to efficiency continues unconsciously in the Western psyche, bearing witness to the shadow side of the current living god, the Economy, the god who continues to urge Western civilization onward by means of ever more efficiency.

GROWTH

If efficiency seems the road to power and the method of maintaining its hold, so growth seems the proof of power. Therapeutic jargon speaks of "inner growth" that leads to psychological maturity and which translates to mean "in control," taking charge of your life, empowered.

Yet when the word "growth" appears, at least six distinct notions converge. They can be put into a list.

1. Increase in size (expansion or getting bigger)
2. Evolution in form and function (differentiation or getting smarter)
3. Progress (improvement or getting better)
4. Conjunction of parts (synthesis, integration or wider networking)
5. Temporal succession in stages (maturation or getting riper, wiser)
6. Self-generation (spontaneity or becoming creative, independent)

These ideas of growth glow with the hope of betterment, although we all know that getting bigger is not always better, that maturation also means withering and dying and that independence also brings solitude.

Nonetheless, growth remains freighted with positive implications like fertility, hope, good health, progress, optimism, strength, invulnerability, conquest and even life itself: "grow or die." The positive implications persist, despite the fact that a countercurrent has been discrediting the idea of growth in recent years. The six main meanings of the term have lost some of their grip. What once was a sacred cow in both psychology and Wall Street can now be dismembered. We can put the dissecting knife to the term, just as government and industry are putting the pruning knife to growth all through their hierarchies. Growth is becoming a more subtle idea than the naive version suited to a child, where indeed getting bigger, getting smart, getting better, etc., has to be the one indubitable path that leads upward and onward. Nowadays "more" can no longer equate with growth because "more" actually can restrict the possibilities inherent in growth.

I like to think that this loss of faith in one of the basic metaphors of the American belief system, that of unending improvement through expansion, could have resulted from the sophistication brought about by psychology. For we know that our individual personal "growth" did not follow the path we imagined as children: constant progress from four, to very nearly five, to six and then on and on to double digits, teens . . . We each know intimately that the psyche grows through defeats, divorces, depressions, and that every change for the better was paid for by concomitant loss.

That the gears are now in reverse cannot all be attributed to psychological sophistication. Quality has been replacing quantity throughout the nation's desire. Wherever we see increase we feel its weight. All the numbers going up no longer portray the optimistic spirit, but instead indicate monstrosities, epidemics, ugliness, future disaster, extinction. Growth has taken on a cancerous tinge. To use the word now sends a message of potential danger, whether the growth be in the debt, the population, the underemployed, the homeless, the dimension of cities, the size of government, the particles in the air, the tax rate, the cost of living, the cholesterol count, even the rising numbers on the bathroom scale. Going up now means decline. What before was the measure of progress has become a sign of problems.

Nowhere is this clearer than in the reversal suffered by the idea of development—a favorite word both in the economics of urbanism and in psychology. Here, psychology lags behind; it still teaches and promotes development.

The basic lessons of developmental psychology come out of the Victorian armoires of social Darwinism and its version of growth: get big, get strong, win out. Progress is a natural process. Don't get left back; take on your problems like a hero and work them through. These ideas teach psychological capitalism: how inferiorities are overcome and impairments integrated into an ever growing ego that is getting it all together. Developed personalities can do whatever they want. They take charge of their fates.

Psychology is no more aware of the shift in value of the idea of development than are landowners and real estate promoters. For today when the rumor spreads that developers are moving in, citizens cringe and protests form. The developer who once was only the improver has now also become the destroyer, and "developed" land means cut trees, bulldozers, access roads and eventually fast food. We no longer are quite sure which term carries the more ecologically negative connotation: underdeveloped or overdeveloped. Maybe it's neither, but rather that same childish view of growth as good.

Critics of growth, from the Club of Rome and E. F. Schumacher to the Zero Population movement and deep ecologists, focus mainly on demographics, social disintegration, exhaustion of natural resources and food supplies and the destruction of habitat and cultures as consequences of uncontained growth. These critiques have fundamentally refined the notion and cautioned its proponents.

But something else is sapping the idea of growth as a healthy solution to the nation's ills. Our hearts have turned in another direction and our heads are following. The lingering aftermath of Vietnam, the diffidence and corruption in high office, the faces of the hungry and the bodies of the dying have shifted our focus. Victorious conquest and the grandiosity of expansionism no longer carry the national honor. Smart bombs do not compensate for dumb kids.

We have begun to consider our losses altogether differently, so that the attitudes in business offices are no longer
as separated as they once may have been from the emotions
in therapy offices. Sitting still, reflecting, remembering,
grieving and giving in now carry the flag forward—because
"forward" is not where it used to be. Going on now
means going downward into the faults of our culture and
backward into the griefs of its memories. Today we need
heroes of descent, not masters of denial, mentors of maturity who can carry sadness, who give love to aging, who
show soul without irony or embarrassment. Mentors, not
cheerleaders; mentors, not boosters or Babbitts. Better
sadness in high places—Lincoln as example—than endemic
depression in the population and the economy. The legendary heroes of the ancient world—Ulysses, Aeneas, Psyche,
Persephone, Orpheus, Dionysos and even Hercules—all
descended into hell to learn other values than those that
rule the daily business of sunlit life. They came back with a
darker eye that can see in a dark time.*

The Vietnam Memorial is black in a dominatingly
white-walled capital. That memorial is dug downward, unlike the aspiring needle of the Washington Monument and
the growth charts whose arrow always goes up. Visitors

---

* For an account of the underworld as a psychological experience, may I refer the
reader to two of my books: *The Dream and the Underworld* (New York: HarperCollins, 1979) and *Suicide and the Soul* (Dallas: Spring Publications, 1976). Most
valuable in this context is Robert Bly's chapter "The Road of Ashes, Descent, and
Grief" in his *Iron John* (Menlo Park, 1990) and Michael Meade's chapter "The
Water of Life" in his *Men and the Water of Life* (New York: HarperCollins, 1993).

today to the political shrines of the nation often aim toward that dark mirror of memory before they climb the stairs and stare up to the oversize images of Presidents in their white Apollonian temples. Can we revise the idea of growth so that the progression it implies can be incorporated into a more matured notion of growth itself? "When I was a child, I spake as a child, I felt as a child, I thought as a child: now that I am become a man, I have put away childish things" (I Corinthians 13:11).

Let me propose, then, a second list of kinds of growth that correlates with some of the changes in both our psychological and historical conditions:

1. Deepening
2. Intensification
3. Shedding
4. Repetition
5. Emptying

1. Deepening: The downward direction cannot simply mean decline, since organic models insist that things can't grow upward unless they grow downward at the same time, like most plants. The downward direction differs from downsizing, because downward refers to depth, to the deepening of feelings and relational insights. Thirty years of self-help, marriage counseling and recovery have been influencing the entire nation toward deepening. Deepening in organizations can take many cues from these lessons in the private sphere without following them literally.

Deepening starts with staying with what is happening, staying in the mess. Staying power. This could translate into staying with the organization and in the job. Career advancement would not require transfer and moving elsewhere to broaden and gain experience (or to get out of the present mess). "Gain" is anyway part of the naive growth model. Deepening insists: no avoidance and no escape. Stay planted. No leave of absence. Clean up the mess. Gary Snyder, the poet and philosopher of Nature, declares that the best way, maybe the only way, to change a situation is to imagine, even to declare, that you will stay where you are, in your locale, the rest of your life.

Deepening forces an organization, like a marriage, to go into itself to get to the bottom of its troubles. Going to the bottom does not stop at the bottom line, but goes into those supporting myths and philosophies on which an organization—again, like a marriage—rests. What will be sacrificed to achieve its aims and to whose cost? What corners is it willing to cut? What deceits does it practice? Can it ever be content, or must it be perpetually under pressure for ever more growth, called success?

Eventually, deepening gets down to bedrock ideas and the moral grounds which, like marriage, make partnership in the organization possible. Does this organization have a fundamental vision which I can share; does it desire the same goals; do we practice similar principles? What, truly, realistically, are its principles—and what are mine? Are we joined in a marriage for money? Is our partnership a utilitarian relationship—that is, are we useful to each other, and therefore do I use the business as it uses me? The more I stick with these issues and the more the organization can stay with its own self-questioning depths, the more both I and it may be actually growing (in the sense of growth as evolving and maturing). This growth could be called growth of soul.* As in a garden or a marriage, deepening brings ugly twisted things out of the soil. It's a work in the dirt.

2. Intensification in economics refers mainly to those kinds of production that use lots of hands, like intensive farming on small paddies and terraces by peasants as opposed to extensive agriculture over thousands of acres by harvesting machines. I want rather to import the idea of intensification not from the economics of labor but from the mental work of poetry.

Poets in German are called *Dichters* and a poem is a *Gedicht,* a *Dichtung. Dicht* means thick, dense, so that *verdichten* means to thicken, condense. Poetic language intensifies by packing lots of implications and references into the small space of a word or a phrase. A poem miniaturizes. It is like a computer chip or an optic fiber that carries many messages simultaneously. Such are metaphors.

---

* For expositions of making soul in daily life, see two books by Thomas Moore, *Care of the Soul* and *Soul Mates,* both published by HarperCollins.

However, so long as we have not shed the mentality of the child, we tend to be more impressed by expansion. We are a nation with a fondness for grandeur, the biggest cave, the widest canyon, the tallest building. One of the characteristics of an American is this romantic predilection for immensity. Intensification goes against the national grain. We can make a comparison with the Japanese psyche, of which it is said, and by the Japanese themselves, that they have invented little. They only made things smaller; for example, the fan, invented in China, but folded and pleated first in Japan.

Corporations intensify by squeezing more return from each hour of labor, each tiny TV bite, each linear foot of marketing space, each dollar of capital investment. They aim to tighten up and crowd more into a single unit. From one perspective this is economic, from another it's poetic.

Going about reductions, cost cutting and doubling up on jobs inspired by a lean-and-mean philosophy isn't the same as intensification in the discipline of art. If it's art, then the intensification must be measured by benchmarks of another kind—that is, quality rather than efficiency. Long-lasting value rather than immediate profitability. A cost-benefit analysis of the labor of art might have to declare it a total loss—or an astounding value-added product (burlap, bottle caps, scrap wire and black acrylic from the hand of a painter who becomes "hot" owing to the efforts of a Manhattan gallery). What makes art compressed is neither the frugal use of materials nor hastening the time of production.

Although business and art both use intensification to achieve their ends, their philosophies widely differ. Whereas business cuts for efficiency, the arts use similar procedures for complexity, meaning and beauty. Could business continue its methods of intensifying but shift the philosophy which the method serves? Could we imagine business tightening and condensing to enhance the beauty of its performance, to offer more interesting complexity to its staff and customers, to contribute meaning to the world it serves? This aesthetic approach offers a more subtle meaning to the idea of growth than simple expansion and suggests the incorporation of values other than those measured by the corporate financial officer.

What counts in art's intensity is the artist's dedication, passion, enthusiasm, ecstasies and sweat. There is a devotional focus to what you are doing—an intensive concentration that seems like obsession to some who declare you a workaholic or job-possessed, especially by those possessed by "family values." But nothing intensifies more than being in love—the love brought to the art of your work and the love in which the work is done. Nothing makes one leaner either, for the whole psyche is concentrated upon the object of desire. Lean, yes, but not mean.

3. Shedding: The customary metaphors of shedding come from the cycle of nature and they feel comfortable: the fall of autumn leaves, serpents slipping their skins, crustaceans leaving their hard carapaces in order to grow larger and the old habits humans renounce on New Year's Day. Other sheddings are less comfortable. They hurt: the pink slip, the closing of a unit or a department, the removal of an entire assembly plant to foreign shores. In both these sheddings, one brought about by necessities of nature and the other justified as economic necessity, only extrinsic activities have been shed. The corporation may cut the payroll by a thousand and the government disband some programs but the intrinsic viability of the whole is not fundamentally touched. The snake, in fact, is now in better shape.

I want rather to suggest *intrinsic* shedding, not a reduction of frills and perks, not just letting go of nonessentials for the sake of renewal. It's easy to cut fat, especially pork. I mean radical shedding. I take my model again from depth psychology rather than from the cyclical revitalization of nature or from the sort of puritan asceticism that enjoys tightening the belt every now and then and that witch-hunts business, government, research and academic institutions with ethical-cleansing fervor. I am not trying to redeem the pain and loss of shedding by tying it to efficiency, productivity or hope in future growth.

Radical shedding happens in those crises that move in on the soul and cannot be easily fixed. They come often unannounced, at any time, especially as one hits midlife. They may have a specific and immediate cause, such as bankruptcy, divorce, illness; or no apparent cause at all.

The very essence of one's organized life is suddenly under fire, or swamped. Like a natural catastrophe.

Can we think in a similar way about shedding essentials in an organization? Can a corporate organization, like a human life, go through a similar sort of shattering insecurity, reevaluation of purpose, decline in self-esteem? Can the organization's identity be placed in question, the principles that govern its daily activities, the accountability of its accounting procedures—that is, the values by which it takes stock of itself? Can it examine ruthlessly its direction, its relations with employees, the public and the environment? Can all that it conceives to be its individuality be shed? Not literally, of course, even if most seriously, just as the crises that assail the individual person are most serious though they do not entail a literal jump from the Golden Gate Bridge. But they do demand radical shedding of those identities to which one is unquestioningly attached.

Think of shedding in terms of the ugliness of rigorous clear-cutting rather than just cleaning up the undergrowth. Or think of it as a forest fire. The catastrophe model does not intend something better, some future growth, although we like to soften the blow by predictions of a positive outcome. I am reaching here for kinds of crises beyond the familiar ones business must face: relocation, incompatible mergers, lawsuits, wholesale desertions, pirating, patent infringements, delayed start-ups, stockholders' rebellion, cost overruns, fraud, embezzlement and so on. I am trying

to describe an organization's soul crisis which has no defin-
able cause and therefore cannot be dealt with expeditiously
and resolved. This essential shedding seems to be a kind of
autonomous natural process of disorder and decay affecting
the soul in a corporate body just as it does in a human
body. The crisis which forces shedding also forces a philosophical re-visioning, as if the crisis were demanding a
discrimination between what must be held and what can be
let go, a paring down to the bare-bone reasons this organization exists. Sometimes management tries to head off
these breakdowns by means of group retreats, psychological consultants or open sessions aiming to reformulate the
mission statement. They may not work because the timing
is off—preemptive becomes premature, abortive, if it is
not in tune with the seasons of the soul.

What makes shedding so difficult is fear. Like a person, an organization accumulates systems, equipment, procedures, sections—all sorts of redundancies to protect it
from the naked fear that it might be steering a wrong
course, or worse, failing. So the task of shedding is much
like facing the fears in therapy. It is a task of imagination.
A patient worries that her husband will leave her; another
worries that he is becoming impotent; a third fears going
crazy; another believes he has cancer. Therapy says to each
of these fears: "Go on." What would it be like to lose
your husband, to be impotent, to go crazy, to have cancer?
Follow the morbid fear, the irrational fantasy. Take imaginative risks; or as Robert Jay Lifton, the eminent psycholo-

gist who has studied holocausts and catastrophes, says, the task is to imagine the real, or to imagine as realistically as possible the consequences of shedding, to visit with the mind the scenarios of catastrophe and letting go of all security structures, comforting identities, realized achievements, forward planning. See what remains, for only what remains can be truly relied on for growth.

4. Repetition has long been a bugaboo of industrial mass production, supposedly turning humans into machines as in Chaplin's *Modern Times*. But for all the advancement of robotics in factories and electronic processing in offices, the repetitious work of the production line still turns out the goods America consumes. Just think of Chinese and other East Asian assembly stations, or the chicken dressers and migrant farm laborers that give us our daily bread.

Growth carries a positive sign because it is dynamic and organic like a tree, whereas repetition is considered negative because it is static and inanimate like a machine. Freud, too, put repetition on the side of death, seeing the compulsion to repeat as the primary activity of the death instinct. Our common notions of repetition are so haunted by horrible fantasies of deathlike machines that we visualize, as in the movies, the organic life of beetles, ants and cockroaches as kinds of machines whose main fearful characteristic is repetitive motions. (For a far more subtle analysis of machines, beginning with the very first machine— the Egyptian social, political and religious structure that

could construct the pyramids without actual machinery—
see Lewis Mumford's great work, *The Myth of the Machine.*)

Let's think about repetition from another, less offen-
sive angle. Repetition is fundamental not only to machines;
it is the fundamental method in both ritual and the arts.
Instead of a drive toward death, the compulsion to repeat
is an instinct toward art. It shows the soul's pleasure in
practice, in polishing, in precision.

Something in human nature demands performing in
exactly the same way again and again, like the rituals that
greet the sun or those that put the children to bed with the
same story told with the same inflections, night after night.
It's practicing your golf swing or the catcher's throw to
second base—over and over again. We become artists only
when we enjoy the practicing as much as the performing.
Until then we are caught by the limelight rather than the
art. It's not the opening in the gallery that makes the
painter (although it may make his or her career); it's
the repetitious actions in the studio. Over and over again,
not to get it finally right, not for the sake of perfection, but
simply doing it as if for its own sake, freed from *having* to
do it. The work working by itself, mechanically, repeti-
tiously, impersonally.

Could this idea of disinterested repetitiveness—one
of the highest aims of Zen, mystical contemplation and
religious practice, as well as the practice of the arts and
sports—transfer to administration, sales, production, accounting? We cannot begin to imagine how this transfer

might affect these activities until we at least entertain the idea of repetition as the essence of craft. Why not imagine all the repetitive unprofitable actions of sales calls, number crunching and office forms as essential to the craft of business, not as undignified routines but as modes of care for accuracy and as signs of vocation. Then repetition will be conceived not as a compulsion, a slavelike dehumanizing burden, but as the way things become beautiful. Does this help to understand the interlocking connections of the Japanese between their mechanical repetitive style of work, their sense of ritual and beauty and the quality of their product?

5. Emptying: Let me draw your attention to a very different notion of growth that seems almost its contrary. I place its start with Goethe and see parallels with Buddhist thinking. Goethe's examination of leaf growth in plants confirmed his intuition that the shape of the plant as a whole was determined in some way by the negative space around which the leaves unfold. Let's say that the leaf doesn't just push its way into optimal expansion and round itself out, occupying the most space possible for absorption of sunlight. If this were the case, then all leaves would take on the same round shape. No. The leaf takes on the specific shape of oak, maple or serrated cut-leaf birch because something in the surrounding emptiness governs the leaf's shaping into a species-specific manner. It's not all in the genetic code; or, let us say, the genetic code unfolds in response to emptiness.

Goethe's ideas about plants, whether botanically accepted or not, nonetheless invite our attention to what is
not there. Even further: what is not there characterizes the
particular nature of each kind of plant. This idea claims
that emptiness has an invisible power that plays a determining role in what appears. Patterns emerge and grow out of
the empty, much as the potter's jar forms itself around the
active presence of a hollow. Each container—pot, vase,
jug, cup—is simply the external shell of a specifically
shaped void. The power is in the void. That nature abhors a
vacuum may be only a modern Western idea of nature.
Different schools of Buddhist thought, for instance, consider the seeds of all existing things to be contained in a
substratum void, so that care for emptiness is what allows
the seed to emerge. Absence takes precedence over presence, or better said, is the first form of presence.

The Italian thinker Gillo Dorfles presents similar
ideas regarding music. The toneless pause between notes
makes the rhythm and melody possible. Music is the result
of specifically spaced and timed moments of silence. Dorfles transfers this idea of the interval to all kinds of motions, including factory work, and the process of thinking
itself in which the empty moment originates the shape of
things to come. Growth would focus on the not-yet, the
voided out, the empty—those places in a day which are
not filled, like the empty page in the schedule book, the
vacant moments in the production line we now would
eliminate as "waste." Instead, they might better be called,

as in music, "rests." They are starts as well as stops; not breaks; empties.

We can apply these ideas of emptying to the aging of people and of systems. Then we would understand the decline and shrinkage that accompanies aging as "value-added" rather than as literal loss. The forgetful mind and lapses of attention, the vague fumbling of motor skills, the closing down of feeling responses and impoverishment of language may not be only as they seem to young eyes. Perhaps space is being made, the rest for a different music, a voiding of the usual for the sake of the unusual.

Similarly with aging business, "downsizing" far-flung conglomerate enterprises, selling off divisions, sunsetting worn-out programs, pulling in the outposts of ambitious hopes and stocking up the larder for pension plans—these events reported in the business news are of course metaphors for older age in men and women. More than that, these events can be imagined as the opening of gestalts from their habitual frames into new and untried spaces. An experiment is going on. To read these processes as signs of contraction and decay forgets one of the oldest ideas in the world, ideas of how the world itself "grew" into being: *creatio ex nihilo,* creation out of nothing. What comes first is nothing.

This view, as I said, accords so well with some Eastern philosophies that we are again brought to realize that ideas serve archetypal powers: the Western idea of growth as I presented in the first list above suits the child, while the one of Goethe, Dorfles and Buddhism suits the aged *senex*. Again my point is simple: we cannot view anything except through archetypal glasses. What is growth to the "wisdom of the East" looks like pathological decay to the archetypal vision of the developing child. What to the optimistic naturalism of the child looks like healthy expansion of networking and improved facility seems to the octogenarian foolish distraction, a disintegration into what Oriental philosophy calls the "ten thousand things," a cancerous metastasis of proliferation.

What I am calling the "archetypal perspective of the developing child" lies at the root of the heroic growth idea; for heroes—Moses, Jesus, Hercules, Perseus, David, Oedipus—begin as endangered, vulnerable, abandoned infants or children. Bigger = Better offers a grandiose defense that seems to protect against, even overcome, the inherent insecurity at the heart of heroic strength.

If our national notion of growth remains tied to the archetypal perspective of the child and therefore blinded to more complex sophisticated kinds of growth, then the emphasis by the psychology industry on the "inner child" and on personal childhood sufferings supports the very archetype that determines the nation's naive ideas of growth. To keep the economy growing and the country moving forward into another century requires not only passing through the ending of this one but also *a stance that welcomes endings*. I like to remember Ulysses in the *Odyssey*, who wants only to put an end to his twenty-year career of wandering by finally coming home. Homer's whole epic is dedicated to the end. And I think of Prospero in Shakespeare's *Tempest,* who finally is able to put away his magic, break his staff and drown his book, welcoming the end.

Endings do not belong to the consciousness of the child; the child looks forward. And the first of these endings is putting closure on American childlikeness itself (which does *not* imply tough-minded, hard-hearted, unimaginative "realism"). To open the next century, we shall go through—in fact are already going through—the rituals of closing this one, the memorials of loss, the mournings and the remorse for having held too long to the childish kinds of growth that indeed "made this country great"— but not only great. Growth now and to come will depend less on what programs we initiate to bring about growth during this closing time than on how this closing time helps refashion the idea of growth itself.

Therefore this chapter has elected to retain the idea of growth rather than to reject it whole hog. However, we have tried to rework "growth" by separating it from the childish innocence and simplistic optimism which have led its main critics to belittle growth in favor of limits, smallness and no-growth, zero-sum models. I do not believe that these critics have struggled enough with the idea itself, and so their dismissals do not satisfy the deep human wish that the term "growth" symbolizes. To discard the idea only represses this archetypal desire and leaves it still encased in childish simplistics.

I have been trying a different approach. Rather than exchanging growth for no-growth, I am adding to the list of notions with which this chapter began. I am filling in the shadow of these notions, by taking the idea of growth into profounder regions of intensification, repetition, deepening, shedding and emptying. When growth takes on these further meanings which darken its innocence, it is no longer incompatible with the actualities of America's demographic, social and psychological conditions. Then our difficult, even tragic, individual, corporate and national dilemmas can be understood as necessary to the loss of addictive optimism and to the growth of soul. And we can encourage growth's own maturation into a more fully formed and subtly differentiated idea that comes provided with its own inhibiting limits even as it remains a term of inspiration.

SERVICE

By proposing that we alter our perspective on efficiency and growth, I am aiming to take down the old heroics of business as battle, conquest, victory and reward, and their shadows, passivity, imprisonment, defeat and loss. I am seeking to adapt to the actualities of a coming century in which another sort of courage, another style of enterprise will have to obtain: a style that is also heroic but cast in another mold. To be bold and brave, to set forth into unknown country, to rescue the endangered city, may mean taking the risk of letting go of the old ideas of heroics, such as going it alone, keeping others in line, stonewalling and wielding a ruthless ax. If the GNP of the United States has shifted from the heroics of production to a primarily service economy which provides, it is said, 100 percent of all new jobs, then we have to do some serious reevaluation of service. Yet the very idea of service stands in the way of optimizing service itself.

Service offends deep strata of human dignity. We may all want service, but who wants to give it? For service still means *menial* service (not banking, brokering, telephoning, teaching, installing, diagnosing or writing). The first trouble lies in the word, which invites in its cousins—serf, servile, servant, servitude, servility, all descendants from the common Latin ancestor, *servus,* slave. Service, as it is defined in our culture, is hardly empowering, or empowering only to those persons who can command service and the system for which we slave. Political promises to get the country moving again cannot be delivered unless the service sector delivers good service. But what is good service? How can we think about a service economy if the idea echoes back to a slave economy?

From what we have just seen in regard to efficiency, we cannot improve service merely by making it more efficient—that is, fast, frictionless and fault-free. If that was all there was to improving service, then reliable digital equipment, optic fiber, satellites, robots, software—in other words, more productive impersonal systems (gas chambers and cremation ovens?)—would take care of the problem. In fact, the personal factor would be more and more eliminated—but then what about "jobs"?

Moreover, can improved systems of service delivery, better hardware and software, alone improve the quality of service? When a restaurant owner puts in a second door side by side with the sole existing one between dining room and kitchen, thereby facilitating single-direction traffic through each door, he is probably making faster, and less subject to friction and fault, the delivery of food to table and bussing dishes to washer. But does this necessarily improve the quality of relations between diner and waiter? In Stangl's camp there were great technological refinements; using the goals of fast, frictionless and fault-free, Treblinka provided superb service. Ingenuity, technical efficiency, impersonal objectivity may implement delivery, but do they complete the picture of good service? Are there benchmarks? Models?

Good service as measured by the standards of the well-heeled elite moves away from impersonal delivery toward a more personal and individualized touch. A concierge on each hotel floor, private hospital room with private nurse, more attendants per passenger in first-class air travel, chauffeured car or valet parking, a flow of personal hands-on attention: decorators, hairstylists, tailors, masseurs, financial planners. Good service by this standard simply wants "someone to talk with who can do well, and respectfully, what I ask for." Notice the five components in this definition: a human person, with language skills and sensitivity, adequate to the task, as judged by the recipient or customer. This is a far cry from automatic electronic devices. So which way do we go in thinking about service: more systematized or more personalized?

According to the Swedish thinker Evert Gummesson,* the main mistake in all thinking about service is that we are hardly thinking about it at all. The first research centers focusing on the subject in business and public af-

---

* Evert Gummesson, "Service Productivity: A Blasphemous Approach," Dept. of Business Administration, University of Stockholm, 1992; and "Can Implementation Be Taught?" ibid., 1991.

fairs were started only in the mid-eighties (Karlstad, Sweden, and Arizona State, Tempe), so that *most ideas of service have been imported from ideas of production,* as if good service could be defined by criteria of productivity.

I am contesting this approach with all the vigor I can muster by drawing an exaggerated opposition between productivity and service. They need to be kept clearly distinct because they grow out of fundamentally different psychological attitudes, even archetypally different styles of existence. Our habitual ideas insist that to serve is closer to surrender; to produce, more like conquering. Production masters material; service submits to it. In the language of myth, our ideas of productive employment indicate the influence of Prometheus, the Greek Titan, upon the do-it-yourself ego, or of Hephaistos, the Olympian craftsman and arms maker, because production constructs: whereas service employment, because it protects, conserves and furthers, more likely indicates Hestia, the Goddess of the hearth. She is almost invisible in her service, although instrumental in maintaining the daily round. Or our idea of service could also be more Hermetic, after Hermes, the God and master of media and mediation, because service deals, exchanges and communicates messages impersonally without involvement in the message itself.

Gummesson's main complaint is that to think adequately about service, we must free it from the productivity paradigm. Moreover, we must first recognize how entrenched we are in the paradigms that have worked so well so far, even when these paradigms force services on the recipient who feels these innovations as impositions.

Here I am referring to service that anticipates needs for a product, even invents needs, entrapping the consumer into wanting what he does not need. Good service becomes defined as delivery of product that links, or chains, the consumer to the production facilities and their over-capacity. Production, rather than scaled to meet the needs of the market and harnessed by these actual needs, sets the pace, requiring the market to serve the needs of production. Good service can hardly be defined by delivery of product without the consuming population being thrown into an Orwellian nightmare of forced consumption trying to satisfy the increase of invented needs. ("You can never get enough of what you don't really want," said Eric Hoffer.) In short, the production model of thinking about service serves consumption (as a last stage of the production process), but not the consumer.

Because we have had more than a hundred and fifty years of rapid, innovative, technological solutions that improve service delivery, we continue to imagine along the same paths, sometimes deaf to suggestions that service can improve by nontechnological means. The old cliché holds: new wars are fought with the last war's weapons and by the last war's generals. Past ideas that once worked determine approaches to new problems.

As service machines replace physical labor—washing clothes, washing cars, washing floors—and as computer chips and software replace mental labor, our ideas of service remain tied to labor-saving devices. At the same time, surplus and inadequately paid labor have become the major concerns of futurists as well as the major parasite sucking the vitality of Western capitalism.

In the 1950s the Western idea of an efficient steel mill employed the fewest people per ton of product: in China the most efficient steel plant gave the most employment and had the highest ratio of persons per ton. Today we may be tilting toward that Chinese thinking as employment becomes as important as productivity for the well-being of the nation. And it is in the service sector where the new jobs are found even as the imagination of that sector remains fastened to the old paradigms of productivity.

Because the imagination of business and industry remains under the spell of the productivity paradigm, a paradigm that favors high tech/low touch employment, we continue to devalue the obverse side of the coin so necessary for service: high touch/low tech. And so our society continues to foment an underrewarded, disrespected, resentful and recalcitrant workforce, waiting for the lottery to lift them from the degradation inherent in the very idea of their jobs. So long as good service means "eliminating what does not need to be done" (the "form follows function" theory of modernist architecture applied to human services), we will have barren no-frills service stripped of fantasy, restricting the imaginative power in those who serve. Good service "takes the extra step," "goes out of its way," shows imaginative variations, finds precise ways of pleasing. It calls on imagination and delights the imagination as well as the senses. It is more Baroque than Bauhaus.

To move our ideas of service, we will have to clear away the usual discourse obsessively focused on delivery, implementation, rationalization and performance, with models drawn from McDonald's quick-serve systems and Federal Express's quick telephone response rule. The reduction to simplistics of the human delight in serving—caring, mending, nursing, teaching, cleaning, answering, helping, fixing, greeting, conserving, easing, feeding, leading—can only vitiate all our attempts at quality improvement on which the economy depends.

What after all is "quality" but the approximation to an ideal—that is, the idea of quality closes the gap between an actual material event and an idealized perfect form. By aiming at perfection, quality reminds the soul of ideal beauty. "Perfect service," we say. A quality chemical has not been degraded by substitutes, attempting to be 100 percent pure. A quality machine tool tolerates only microdimensional imperfections. A quality service brings otherworldly expressions of praise: superb, graceful, beautiful, divine, marvelous, wonderful. As an *aesthetic* gesture, good service pleases both giver and recipient by the beauty of the performance, thereby enhancing life and adding value to an event that would otherwise be only a trans-action.

This aesthetic idea of quality offers a different base for the acknowledged superiority of Japanese quality. I believe we have wrongly attributed that superiority to a set of economic and psychological factors only: the conformity of their workforce and the homogeneity of their population; their intense school pressure assuring habits of concentration and long attention span; their management-labor teamwork; their disciplined competitiveness from top to bottom; their traditions of obedience to rules (specifications), even to their "shame culture," in which errors become psychologically intolerable.

To these factors supposedly accounting for Japanese quality, I would add their aesthetic sensibility that is essential both to the decorum of Japanese daily life and to the complexities of their imagistic language. From the beginning, the Japanese mind is set in a culture that pays devout attention to sensate details. Their hobbies in the refined arts—flower arrangement, tea ceremony, calligraphy, martial arts and weapons, miniaturization, painstaking handcrafts, garden appreciation, food preparation, traditional dance—as well as the subtle infinitesimal variety of gestures in the Noh performances bespeak a "precision consciousness" of sensate aesthetic qualities in an attempt at the ideal. Precision consciousness is what we call "quality control."

Of course, this objective, aesthetic impersonality can

lead to empty formalism and the stultifying stiff mannerism that Americans see all too often in Japanese procedures. Any mode casts its shadow. I am not suggesting that we imitate the Japanese mode of service because it is better. I am rather suggesting that we notice that Japanese delivery of quality results from a precision consciousness based in an aesthetic tradition.

Quality service, then, enhances life by keeping one eye always on the ideal, striving for the purity of perfection. Of course, the ideal cannot be achieved, for that is the nature of "ideal," which explains why an ideal is not simply a benchmark standard. "Ideal" implies qualities that are beyond any preset description. They are only pointers to how things should be and, perhaps, how they desire to be, as if something in each moment of life wants to transcend itself. Perhaps improvement is not only a human desire. Perhaps progress toward perfection, toward the realization of the ideal, is inherent in the very nature of things, which service recognizes by doing what it can to support this desire for enhancement, bringing out of each thing its best possible performance. This is the spiritual impulse that is the true root of service. Our service in life and our service to life attempt to return whatever we do to a utopic vision, the ideal of heaven, which each of us feels in the heart as an aesthetic joy whenever something is done really right.

In recent years service has been imagined more in human than in heavenly terms. Quality service has more and more come to be defined as "personalized service." This is due to the influence of therapeutic psychology with its needling insistence on personal feelings and personal relationships, a focus that disturbs the formal codes of conduct in business affairs. For business observes rituals that serve the task and the organization impersonally—cold, uncaring and patriarchal as that may seem.

When personalized service becomes the criterion of quality service, then more attention is paid to the relationship between receiver and provider than to the objective nature of the task. "Would you do this for me?" says the cabin attendant, asking me to pull my seat to an upright position for landing. Why do it for her? As a favor? As a personal kindness? Instead, we are performing the impersonal rituals of landing, the correct procedures that approximate an ideal form and have little to do with the human relations between her and me. The waiter's name does not bear upon the dinner for which I came to the restaurant—I'm not there to make his acquaintance. His concern for my dining will be shown neither by his imperative, "enjoy," as I begin, nor by his interrogation about the dishes afterward, but by his precision consciousness regarding each and every act, the rituals that he is there to perform, thereby doing his job beautifully.

Personalized service puts the person before the service. One person serves the other; I am in service to you, or you to me, so that the master/slave situation of servile servitude immediately lurks in the shadow, splitting surface sweetness on the one hand and aggressive resentment on the other. Only a saintly Sister of Charity can perform personalized service without being caught by the suppressed hostility emanating from this shadow.

It is the job that demands service; the objectivity of the job turns service into a ritual activity. Then we might regard service as less for the sake of a person than for a thing, an event or situation, less a disempowering servitude than an enhancement, less a subjective kindness than an objective ritual. Like waxing the floor to enhance its luster, like airing a room after everyone else has gone to bed.

By objective ritual, I mean the way a nurse bathes an immobile patient, a priest says Mass, an interpreter translates the text, an actor plays the part. In each of these cases the personal may interfere with the objective performance of the service and the specifications of the job. Not only persons call for service; their things do, too—the oil changed, the VCR cleaned, the dryer repaired, the message transmitted. Ceremonies of the repairman. Objects have their own personalities that ask for attention, just as the ads show the smiling bathtub that enjoys the new cleanser or the wood siding that likes the fresh stain which protects it from decay. Treating things as if they had souls, carefully, with good manners—that's quality service.

We have now sailed by, rather scornfully, the two main lines of discourse regarding service; the first, with reference to the deliverer's performance (the high-tech production model), and the second, with reference to the recipi-ent's satisfaction (the model of personalized needs). We have left the arguments and measurements of delivery, sat-isfaction, performance, personal and impersonal altogether in order to return to where this chapter began. Let's look again into the old idea of service that is so abhorrent: service as servitude, inescapable bondage unto death. Not to a technical system of productive efficiency (Stangl; and also what Japanese youth are beginning to rebel against), and not to a personal customer who is always right (He-gel's "master" become the consumer whose every wish one must obey). Rather, an idea of servitude to the Other, the Other as the planet as a whole and in each of its smallest components.

The idea of service that I am imagining would derive from deep ecology. The Gaia hypothesis holds that our world, this planet, is a breathing organism. It is all and everywhere alive and enjoys degrees of consciousness, where consciousness is no longer defined as an exclusive property of human beings and so no longer restricted to location only inside human skins and skulls. Although the Gaia hypothesis is recent and uses biological, physical and chemical evidence, the idea is as old as the pre-Socratic philosophers, Stoic cosmology, the Neoplatonic world soul (anima mundi), the universal dreaming Soul of Leibniz, and is founded in strata of myths of the earth which the name Gaia, Greek earth Goddess, deliberately indicates.

The careful reader will already have noticed, and perhaps been disturbed by, a characteristic of this book's style which reflects the Gaia hypothesis. The aberration endows all sorts of nouns with subjectivity. You have been reading sentences that attribute consciousness and intention, power even, to ideas, to things and especially to words. Words are given biographies, the book is said to have a task, and phenomena are described as displaying themselves without me or anyone else doing it for them. The book shares the power of agency between the human as subject of the sentences and other kinds of subjects that in most prose, other than children's books and science-fiction fantasy, are not entitled to the right to life. The very way the sentences are composed attempts to liberate the idea of soul from confinement in the human person, especially the first person singular, "I."

Service to a world ensouled implies that human life serves inescapably this large organic system. Our exhalations, our excreta, our emotions—whatever we humans generate—serve in one way or another this interdependent complexity we call the biosphere, and which other cultures describe with the names of powers, gods and goddesses. As servers in this organism we are inevitably both providers and recipients. Good service would be defined by estimations of what's good for the world's soul and bad service by what is neglectful and diffident.

These estimations of what is good or bad for the world of course cannot be objectified. Who can say accurately that a disposable diaper serves the world's soul better than a cloth one. How to weigh the water and detergent of washing cloth against the manufacture and disposal of plastic? But you can make your choice with the ideal in mind that which way you go will be beneficial ecologically, and not only beneficial to your bank account or your personal convenience. It is not a matter of inventing a new kind of consumers' guide that can estimate with benchmarks from one to ten what is best and worst for the world, but rather of feeling each decision with an ideal in mind so that your choices reflect an ecological consciousness. This means not only what does this product, this activity, this purchase cost me, but what does it cost the world?

Furthermore, as we imagine the human soul to reside within each individual person, so the world soul may be imagined to have its locus in each individual thing. Things then become subjects, too, rather than mere objects. When they are treated as dead objects and left in neglect, they will reveal more and more toxicity. What starts as "user-friendly" begins to emit "bad vibes." How else call our attention to our disservice but for these articles to serve no longer as silent slaves.

This idea of service demands surrender, a continuous attention to the Other. It feels like humiliation and servitude only when we identify with a ruling willful ego as mirror of a single dominating god. But what if a God is in each thing, the other world distributed within this world?

Theology calls this distribution of the divine within

all things the theory of immanence, and, sometimes, pantheism. Whether God is right here in things, whether each thing has its own God, whether there is one God or many Gods, or *any* Gods—these theological questions may fascinate but they are not immediately relevant to the practical point: service treats each particular thing as carrying its own specific value—including that airplane seat which I am asked to place in an upright position. By treating that seat as if it were animated with its own spirit I will be less likely to rough it up and more likely to show care. A cared-for seat will also perform better and provide longer-lasting service.

A theology of immanence means treating each thing, animate and inanimate (perhaps the distinction no longer clearly obtains), natural and man-made, as if it were alive, requiring what each living thing requires above all else: careful attention to its properties, their specific qualities. This plant needs little water; this wood won't bear great weight and burns with a smoky fire. Look at me carefully: I am an aspen, not an oak. Notice differences, pay attention, give respect (re-spect = look again). Notice what is right under your nose, at your fingertips, and attend to it as it asks, according to its needs. Aesthetic sensitivity. Precision consciousness.

These notions of attending and serving are the meanings of the Greek word *therapeia,* from which our word "therapy" comes. The Greek idea of a *therapeutes* was one who attended, was a servant of, and thereby could heal. A service relation to the planet could bring about its healing or at least maintain its health.

An aesthetic idea of service fits with what newer theory calls "high-touch" (rather than high-tech) service. This idea is aesthetic because it requires a sensitivity to the nature of that which is, calling for careful perception and sensitive reactions. These words, "sensation" and "perception," are the English translation of *aisthesis,* which referred in Greek not to some abstract theory of beauty, but to the perception of the sensate world as it appears. I am proposing the idea that service can be relocated from a purely functional concept allied with mechanical efficiency to a qualitative participation of the senses in systemic relations. Service then becomes *fitting ecological response.* Tasks now imagined mainly as duties, or penalties—cleaning up, detoxification, repair, scrubbing, recycling—become models for a therapeutic and aesthetic idea of service.

Suzi Gablik's book on the role of art in an ecologically conscious society describes compassionate action toward things as a new mode for Western art—art in service to the world.* One chapter, describing an artist's devotion to the regular cleaning of the banks of the upper Rio Grande, portrays a ritual of service that is in keeping with a definition of art in its most extreme old-fashioned sense, "art for art's sake," but here no longer a private "creation" by a socially detached elite, separate from life

---

* Suzi Gablik, *The Reenchantment of Art* (New York: Thames & Hudson, 1991).

and the surroundings, but in dedication to life and the surroundings. It is pure art, without compensation. It has no motive beyond the act, no program, no tendentious message—for the river cannot be cleaned by one person, if ever cleaned at all. It is ritual gesture, meditative devotion and service for its own sake, unprofitable and pleasing no customer.

We are now past conflicting definitions of our topic: one measured by corporate profitability, the other by consumer satisfaction, and have landed on a wider shore. Here I would risk defining service with two fundamentals: first, as *harmlessness;* second, as *enhancement.* The best service does the least harm and enhances as value or beauty. It offers the least possible offense to the gods in its performance, its materials and its purpose. Such service follows the ancient medical caution *primum nihil nocere* (first, to do no harm), allowing us to imagine service as a way of healing the world's ills, which it does by raising the quality of whatever it touches. Such service also fulfills the oldest idea of the Hero who once was imagined to be a person who sought the ideal and whose courage and extraordinary gifts were in service to the Gods for the welfare of the community.

MAINTENANCE

One particular application of service constantly calls for attention: maintenance. The idea of maintenance itself needs maintenance, since it is easily neglected when we address the big ideas of changing consciousness for a new century of organizational management. Yet, in the actual budgeting of operational costs—whether a rental property, a hospital, an airport or sports arena, or whether constructing an office building—the maintenance factor carries considerable weight. Even decisive weight. The choice of floorings, the design of windows (sealed or movable), the feel of fabrics, the location of lighting, service elevators, etc., depend on estimated maintenance costs. Future upkeep determines present design. So dominant is this factor in construction, so truly does form follow function, that we seem to be developing a new school of Putzfrau Architecture, buildings designed for or by the cleaning staff. A major contention in the battles between industry and the EPA turn on the costs of maintenance, cleaning up the low maintenance of the past and preventing low maintenance in the future.

Yet low maintenance is highly desirable, not only in

commerce and industry but in every aspect of our lives. As private consumers we want weed-free lawns, dwarf fruit trees, disease-resistant shrubs, artificial mulch, drought-proof plantings, vinyl siding, no-iron cotton, wrinkle-free trousers, ovenproof dishes in self-cleaning stoves. Low maintenance is an ideal of our everyday lives. Systems, plans, constructions and consumer goods that guarantee the least maintenance seem to offer the most efficiency—that is, the least time and labor spent on nonproductive tasks. Our general attitude toward maintenance shoulders it as a burden, not as a value-added improvement. It is merely a repetitive losing battle against deterioration, all things running down and wearing out. So we feel that washing windows, sweeping trash and making beds waste good time that could be spent either productively or leisurely.

This view of maintenance affects the hierarchy of employment categories and wage scales. Maintenance persons are the lowest-paid. This view also affects wider policies of immigration and deeper feelings of racism, even fears of a pariah caste: envisage the convicts clearing the roadsides of your tossed-away cans. The maintenance man and the motel maid belong generally in the unskilled class formed often of immigrants, the impaired, the illiterate and of darker-skinned Americans. Maintenance is therefore an economic question, an ecological question, a sociological question and an issue of justice to people and things.

It is also, importantly, a question belonging to the

conservation of energy and the laws of thermodynamics, principles basic to our physical interpretation of the universe. Let's look at the language for these "low" jobs. We speak of picking up, washing up, doing up, clearing up, tidying up, maintenance as upkeep. Clearly, what is maintained rises up from disorder to order. Maintenance performs a function counter to the one-way direction of entropy down toward meaningless, patternless, random dissociation—like the image of the motel room when checking out. The idea of entropy increase in physics means lowering the grade of a system's energy and corresponds to increased disorder. The end goal is stasis, nothing moving at all. Freud correlated entropy with the death instinct.

Now, if maintenance is basically upkeep, then maintenance shifts the gradient of energy. Science speaks of negentropy, a free energy, that can "rise" above the random force of entropic disintegration. From this standpoint, maintenance as an equivalent to consciousness becomes as creative a factor as production, no longer merely its shadow side, as part of production's "cost." Furthermore, when we look again at the origin of words, "economics" derives from the Greek for housekeeping—*oikos* (house) plus *nomos* (customary order). To follow the word's implication, maintenance becomes a first concern of economic thinking, and low maintenance means simply neglect, leading to decay, disintegration and death.

Even more: besides the economic, environmental,

cosmological and physical questions, our topic can be considered aesthetically. And the aesthetics of maintenance appears once we return this word, too, to its roots, which are *teneo*, I hold, keep (as in "entertain") and *main*, French for hand. Literally, maintaining is hand-holding.

There are two "kinds" of hands like two sides of the brain. One hand holds the reins and steers the wheel. This is the fist of control and the pointing finger of direction. These characteristics belong to the hand that manages— another word from the French and Latin with hand in it. The other hand has to keep in touch, give strokes and have a feel for the job. "Feel," by the way, derives from roots meaning the palm of the hand. Hands-on management may require both the fist and the palm, and attention to maintenance will be integral to two-handed managing.

In preindustrial times and nonautomated societies, hands held huge value in human affairs, not only as implements for "running" labor-saving equipment (a euphemism for handless hurry) but chiefly for contact with elemental things. Handling a problem meant literally that: touching water, wood, embers, ashes, soil, plants, animals, foods, waste and dirt. Hands offered palms up to the Gods or folded in prayer emphasized their place in the order of things. And your life was in your hands, in its lines where your character could be read by a chiromancer. (The word "character" itself derives from the Greek word for engraved lines.) In the hands was a procreative magic, so that the mere touch by the right person in the right way could bless, or heal, or seal a covenant until death, or raise a person from a low station to high. Power was transmitted through the hands.

Sensual delight came back to the one whose hands were into things—the drape of cloth, the balance of a stone, the texture of the soil, the smoothness of a body's skin. A physician knew the condition of things by what they revealed to his hands. As instrumentation advances we no longer give our hands to the things we live and work with all day except at our extremities, digitally, by punching keys, pulling levers, and picking up pieces of paper and plastic packaging. Hands-off production and service has replaced farm hands, field hands, deck hands, handlers of all sorts. Genetic engineering, silicon electronics, biotech and cryogenics, even diagnostics and trading in commodities take place through a glass brightly or by robotics with prosthetic hands. Only our hobbies—gardening, cooking, model building, pet grooming, mending, weaving, needlepoint and a few moments in the week for love's caresses—permit our hands to recover their full employment. But these are moments of leisure; they are not part of business. Is there one piece of new communications equipment you would wish to hold on to through the years because of its friendly feel, apart from the fact that its trade-in price decreases as the next generation of the same item comes on the market?

Low maintenance, like that last stage of consumerism, looting, represents the utterly secular life. No devotion, no ritual attention paid to anything except at the altar of oneself. So we give all our care and concern to treadmills and vitamins, career and accounting, relationships and therapy. Meanwhile we lose the sensuous pleasure things can give us in the frenetic pleasure of acquiring them.

If we lose pleasure by letting go of manual contact, what might things themselves be losing by no longer being held in human hands? Is that perhaps why they seem cursed, not blessed; broken, not healed; thrown away, not kept through life; and why they remain at a lower order— merely unconscious, material, soulless objects? Is that perhaps why we have so much trash because to have is no longer to hold?

Finally, then, and in view of what we have uncovered in the ideas of efficiency and service, maintenance becomes more of a gift than a chore, and disposal more of a giving back than a getting rid. For we can no longer truly get rid of anything, not only because matter can neither be created nor destroyed, only changed, but also because "throwaway" items are now anachronistic. Even impoverished counties, Third World desolations and Native American reservations refuse the refuse. No one will take your garbage anymore.

By "gift" I am saying that maintainance of your property gives pleasure to your neighbor and by maintaining public property you are giving consideration to the fellow citizens who use the same facilities, walk the same side-walks. The attention we give to our property is also a gift to the things themselves, that they not be treated as dirt, mess, waste, slop, crap, junk, rubbish (for those are the trashing insults we use for what we do not want to keep, do not want to touch).

The idea of an *anima mundi* (ensouled world) translates into care for things. Instead of advertising a good product as "untouched by human hands," we now search for things touched by human hands and that are "user-friendly." If things are ensouled, then they too require rituals of disposal which we are beginning to find again in our recycling projects, appropriately called Redemption Centers. Instead of the old punishing puritanical moralisms about dropping litter on the street, we need a new and enjoyable animism that children would be the first to understand. "Don't throw that candy wrapper on the street" —not because it's dirty or bad manners; not because it's wrong; not because "what if everybody did that?"—but instead "because your candy wrapper doesn't want to lie around in the gutter or be stepped on; it wants to be in the trash basket along with all its friends."

When things are not properly buried, cremated or composted, could their souls remain as haunting and poisoning ghosts endangering the community, especially the most vulnerable, the children? Pollution is not only chemical and radioactive. There is psychological pollution, too. Most tribal societies have elaborate taboos to ward off pollution of the soul by invisible spirits in the airs and waters. Our pollutions and toxicities, too, are invisible. Microwaves, high-tension electricity, radon, additives, X rays, lead particles, pesticides—tasteless, colorless, minuscule and seemingly indestructible.

Is our civilization reaping the reward of its disregard for maintenance, which like an implacable revenant is taking its revenge, forcing us to pay anxious attention to even the most infinitesimal residues? The long neglect of things —managing them by discarding them or replacing them rather than caring for them—seems to have resulted in their now asking for another kind of hand, the hand of kindness. Our enormous waste-disposal and cleanup problems have become autonomous powers like destructive zombies exacting tribute for the heaps of ghouls and corpses left around on the victorious battlefields of productivity or dumped in pits and tossed in rivers to be carried away. But there is no "away." Our civilization seems engaged in a heroic ritual of atonement, a propitiation of the spirits. We are attempting to reconcile with invisible powers what low maintenance has neglected, attempting to reconcile in the only atoning ritual a secular economic society understands: gigantic expenditure, the Superfund.

In this Part we have looked at the ideas of efficiency, growth, service and maintenance, intending to probe their meanings and shift their value. Because these ideas so strongly affect our attitudes and the way organizations conduct their business and plan their future, these ideas are powers in their own right. Like four great horses they pull the economic wagon; they are psychologically more influential than the weekly and monthly figures from the Labor Department, the Commerce Department and the Treasury Department. The trade deficit, the gross national product, unemployment statistics, the consumer price index, M-1 and M-2, etc., do not determine actual behavior so much as does the action of our ideas: the worship of growth, the addiction to efficiency, the aversion to service and the disparagement of maintenance. We can now leave our attempt at exposing the power of ideas in order to turn directly to the ideas of power.

2

Styles of Power

The Language of Power

The term "power complex" originates with C. G. Jung and appears largely defined in his *Psychological Types*, first published in English in 1923. The paragraph reads:

I occasionally use this term as denoting the total complex of all those ideas and strivings whose tendency it is to range the ego above other influences, thus subordinating all such influences to the ego, quite irrespective of whether they have their source in men and objective conditions, or spring from one's own subjective impulses, feelings, and thoughts.

In brief, *subordination* of any sort arouses the power complex. The definition implies that to assert self over other, whatever that other may be, puts the other down. The key word in Jung's paragraph is "above." The means to rise above may take many paths. Subordination may use force, strength of will, persuasion by mood, logic of argument, conversion by faith, conviction by reason, terror, manipulation, entanglement or deception. Whatever the method, the power complex subordinates to get and stay on top.

These different modes are familiar enough. Anyone who has lived with a moodily depressed spouse, a cunning manipulator or an ugly bully knows intimately what subordination means, and that the superior position seems mainly to define itself in terms of someone or something else becoming subservient.

We are equally familiar with the techniques of subordination going on in our own character structure—thoughts we will not allow, feelings we prefer to keep down, fantasies and habits that may not see the light of day and are judged straightaway as inferior. Whether inner or outer, in self or in others, Jung's idea of the power complex relies on the idea of a superiorly will-powered ego.

In other places, however, Jung goes beyond ego and speaks of a power drive or instinct to power, appropriating the idea, perhaps from Alfred Adler and perhaps also from Nietzsche's will to power. Jung pairs this power instinct with another overwhelming psychic force, sexuality. He contends that power provides the basis of Adlerian psychology, as sex does Freudian. This contrast goes back further than psychoanalysis, back at least as far as two major sins of church morality in the Middle Ages: *ira* (anger, rage) and *cupiditas* (desire, lust). These anciently sinful passions have now become the power and sexual drives.

Even further back, in the sense of ever-present, stand two mythological figures, Ares/Mars and Aphrodite/Venus. They, too, are often paired and their stories tell about power and sexuality. Behind modern psychological concepts is a long history, and behind the long history are the archetypal configurations which history clothes according to the fashion of the centuries. The archetypal approach to power and sex says that a human being can never quite control either *ira* or *cupiditas* because these explosive drives are where Gods dwell. And though we may think the myths are long forgotten and the Gods and Goddesses dead, they resurrect in the passions of the soul. That our habits are laid out on the lines of mythical grids is an idea that deserves more space and so it will be the focus of Part Three.

Broader than the psychological ideas of power complex and power drive is the word "power" alone, whose rather innocent definition is simply the agency to act, to do, to be, coming from the Latin *potere,* to be able. The ability to perform work: like electric power and muscle power. In fact, power and energy are both abstractions induced from the performance of work. When something moves or changes in any way, we posit, and then measure, the invisible reason for this alteration as energy or power. More broadly still, power can be defined as sheer potency and potentiality, not the doing but the capacity to do.

The study of the word becomes more interesting as we go back to its Indo-European roots. We discover that the word itself invites the psychological meanings given by Jung. "Power" subordinates, indeed! And even without a subject who uses it. No dominant ego need be assumed. For the root of the word is *poti* meaning husband, lord, master; Greek *posis,* husband, from which *des-potes,* "lord of the house" from *domos* (Greek), *domus* (Latin), and *posis,* master. *Dominus* (our dominate, dominant) is the lord, the master, the possessor, and Roman slaves called their master *dominus* as slaves in Greece called their master *despotes* (from which our word "despot").

Already hierarchy and subordination, even despotism, are built into this idea of power. In the Western tradition —expressed in the language we all inherit the moment we speak English (or any other Indo-European-derived language), thereby entering the cultural field of irrevocable and inexorable history—we believe that agency, to do, to act, involves bossing, dominion, lording it over, pushing things, people, the environment around. God himself in the Latin Church is called *Dominus,* and we humble humans made in that image become dominators simply by doing something.

The most perplexing question that runs all through this inquiry into power is: how can we exercise power, do anything at all as agents, without dominating? It is the great question of our historical psyche, perhaps of human nature: how to act without dominion, without oppressive control, and yet accomplish. It is the question that arises in parents raising their children, in social workers helping their clients, in managers giving instructions in an office. Wherever we would do something as agents, power appears, and where power appears so does our Western history in the word. We dominate in the image of our God, *Dominus.*

We can immediately see why political feminism has

focused on hierarchical organization as the keystone of "patriarchal consciousness." Hierarchy subordinates; power becomes domination and despotism. So, dismantle the table of organization and the declension of power downward from above. Restructure, either in utter equality or into flexible, cooperative, leaderless groups—production gangs, assembly teams, task forces—so as to remain horizontal and not pinnacle upward.

For this radical shift in direction, sideways rather than up and down, new sins replace the old. Ruthless leveling—no head dare stick up too high. No one to look up to is the price of not looking down on anyone. Respect, admiration, awe go by the board. Other kinds of conformism and political correctness begin to dominate. A new tyranny emerges: the absolutism of equality.

Besides the archetypal struggle for power between the vertical and horizontal dimensions—now personalized into male versus female—another power struggle goes on within the word itself. The history of the term implicates whatever you do, and however you do it in a dualism of active/passive, master/slave, eventually sadist/masochist. Work can happen only at the expense of power required to move inert matter.

This style of thinking about getting things done follows an ancient Western model of matter as mere potentiality, inert, passive, feminine, void. It must be actualized by something superior to it. Subordination again and again, from Aristotle through St. Thomas Aquinas into Newtonian science. Only very recently will we acknowledge the innate power in matter, that it, too, is energy and that things do not require the dictates of a Caesar to get them moving. Where Caesar appears, there comes the inert crowd, the unmotivated mass. Mastery invites slavery of one sort or another, even if it be only the slavery of the material over which you show your masterful productive dominion. Caesar is called tyrant, ambitious, mighty, master, lord, in Shakespeare's play; these epithets of power at the same time reduce the populace to "You blocks, you stones, you worse than senseless things!" (*Julius Caesar* I, i, 34). The world divides into actives and passives.

The political problems of "crowds and power," as the Nobel Prize-winning writer Elias Canetti described in his classic study, reside in that pervasive idea of power that has Western consciousness in its dominion, an idea which insists that the more lowly and material, the more female and quiescent, the less power; power follows the high road of class, wealth, education, birth or gender. Power stays on top like God in heaven, Moses on Sinai, the Greek Gods on Olympus, Jesus on the Mount of Olives, and raised in resurrection, the colonials over natives, whiteness over darkness, and missionaries on top of their women. The philosophical term is *actus purus,* the most power defined as purest activity. Below is matter, mass, mob—a mere potential needing both to be motivated from its native inertia and yet constrained from spontaneous eruption because of its latent potency. The notion that pure activity is the essence of divinity gives spiritual impetus to the Western worship of productivity, and also to Western machismo, racism, and paranoia.

We can extend the notion of power by investigating beyond the psychological and etymological explorations we have just reviewed and imagining into the common notions that accompany the word. For the term "power" differentiates itself in our minds with a host of shadings in common usage. These different styles of power that we recognize in each other, we also search for or are embarrassed by. I am thinking here of leadership, influence, resistance, authority, tyranny, prestige, control, ambition and the like— aspects of power that we shall soon study. Perhaps these many facets are the components of power, the traits that together compose its force, its ability to act and do, go and get, have and hold, enslave and destroy; perhaps, too, these shadings account for why the idea of power carries such impact and offers such freedom, as well as inflicts such a curse.

As we review the styles of power, we shall mainly be using a *rhetorical method*. How do we speak about power? How does power speak to us, display itself in language? The rhetorical method differs from the usual ones for exposing a subject. The more familiar methods analyze an idea by looking at examples, or they rely on anecdotes, or they deduce logical implications from definitions, or they employ an empirical study of a case from which to draw useful conclusions. Another method, the more moralistic one, divides power into two basic kinds, the good kind and the bad kind, urging one and condemning the other.

A moralistic model appears especially in theories of power. Judgments are disguised under the cloak of theoretical objectivity. Theories present a spectrum of power stretching from influence (good) to coercion (bad), from persuasion (good) to violence (bad), from legitimated (good) to usurped (bad), mandated by symbols (good) or by weapons (bad), shared and relative (good) to despotic and absolute (bad), located in persons or in social structures. Theories usually start with definitions. Definitions set standards, so that ideas of power can then be measured against benchmarks unidimensionally as if on a scale from one to ten. A theory of power tries to treat it as a defined single something.

We need to unpack this difference between definitions and myths since we will be moving back and forth between them all through this book. Using myths as grids lets you analyze phenomena by holding them up against the light of archetypal figures whose attributes and behaviors are even more complicated than what you are examining. Instead of reducing meaning to a definition, myths amplify and complicate. They are the path of richness. Myths add information to phenomena and offer insights. They provide images, puzzles, humor. For instance, the great hero Hercules, a mythical figure who provides a backdrop for much of our male, muscular, untiring, slaughtering, energetic sense of power, was classically called a "beef eater." Lettuce, in contrast, grew in the gardens of Adonis, the smooth-skinned soft-fleshed lover-boy, and lettuce was considered wimpy and negative for virility because it wilted and went limp fast. This pairing of beef and lettuce provides a mythical background to a cultural shift in the malls. Huge hamburgers are yielding space to salad bars. This pairing appears also in comic reverse in the contrast between Popeye who eats spinach for strength and pudgy Wimpy who lives on hamburgers.

In a curious way, myths provide more objectivity than do models of thought. Even though mythical grids use humanlike figures (Hercules) and speak the rhetoric of subjectivity—passions, feelings, habits and attitudes—their effect is more objective because they do not press a theoretical construction upon phenomena. They leave you free to imagine further about meat eaters and vegetarians, about hunters and planters, about changes in pop-culture tastes, about green environmentalism, about "beef" ads, about heroes and power.

The value of a model lies in setting a standard definition useful for measuring approximations to the model. A hero, according to a full and current definition in the Oxford English Dictionary is: "A man who exhibits extraordinary bravery, firmness, or greatness of soul, in connection with any pursuit, work, or enterprise; a man admired and venerated for his achievements and noble qualities."

Rather than an image, a mythical tale or a depiction, we are given a clear objective abstraction. We have a model against which acts, people and qualities can be compared. By setting conceptual measures, a model imposes subtle judgments even as it pretends to objectivity. Is General Norman Schwarzkopf truly extraordinary? If so, to what degree? Has he greatness of soul? Is Muhammad Ali venerated for his achievements and noble qualities? What about Einstein, Eleanor Roosevelt, John Kennedy, Martha Graham, Picasso, Rachel Carson, Lee Iacocca—do they fill the bill? Or a war hero like Sergeant York, an Olympic hero like Mark Spitz or Jesse Owens? We find ourselves measuring, comparing, arguing, dissenting—and especially moralizing about what person, what achievement measures up to the model. Myths don't have this effect. They make us wonder, question and imagine. To take Jesus as model leads to the *imitatio Christi* and the guilt of never measuring up. To take Jesus mythically leads to mystery.

The mythical approach to our subject, power, means that moralizing about it falls away. This is because the background figures of power—heroes, kings, giants, ogres, queens, witches, wise women, crones, spirits, daimones and especially Gods and Goddesses show that there are no absolute good or absolute evil figures. Any God or Goddess can be an enemy and a killer. Any form of power can be destructive or constructively valuable. There are abuses of magnanimity and nurture as there are instances of constructive well-being under the harsh rule of tyranny. Yes, there are even benign despots. A benign despot is not an oxymoron: Western history is filled with constructive monsters like the czar who built St. Petersburg, or Napoleon. The bountiful king binds his subjects by his gifts as does the CEO by the opportunities he offers. The good mother provides and foresees and her sons and daughters become more and more passive and dependent, drinking themselves to death. Benign despotism—isn't that what's feared by those who attack the welfare state?

You will find another major difference between what we are doing here and usual critiques and theories of power. The various styles will not be lined up on any systematic thread of theory, from major to minor, from stronger to weaker, from older to newer, etc. We are not laying out kinds of theory but kinds of power. Rather than a *theory* of power, ours is a *phenomenology* of power, even a phenomenology of the fantasies of power. *Phainomenon* = "that which appears to the sense or the mind." How things show themselves; how they light up (with a root in flashing, shining, revealing).

A phenomenology also supposes that there is no such thing as power per se. It is not an *is,* or as Gertrude Stein said of Oakland, "there is no there there." A phenomenology of power shows no substance with borders that can tell you where power begins and where it leaves off, when it is present and when not. Instead of a sharp definition, we have a family of resemblances (Wittgenstein) among closely related notions and descriptions. A phenomenology of power treats the topic as a bundle of fantasies, of events moving through the mind and the world, the two rather indistinguishable from each other, a protean shape-shifting, requiring lots and lots of terms to grasp the cluster of notions that our language speaks of as signs of power.

Whatever the method—logical, empirical, phenome-nological—we have to use language. A method persuades us by the power of its language, its rhetoric, defined as "the art of persuasion." Therefore, if we can get at the ideas embedded in the language about power, unpack the persuasive ideas that affect our thought and behavior, we shall be as close as we can get to knowing the components of power. All day long, terms like "control," "prestige," "ambition," "charisma," "authority" cross our lips with-out much thought and enter into judgments that determine our decisions, and our relations with colleagues. Since lan-guage is our luggage it's useful to open these terms for inspection. Perhaps we'll find smuggled hypotheses and hidden prejudices, but also long-forgotten values we did not know we were carrying.

While psychologies of all sorts are actively concerned with "empowerment" and use the term regularly in con-ferences and programs, there remains a strange discomfort with the idea of power, not only for the tyrannical implica-tions we have uncovered but for yet another reason. A saying of Jung's expresses this best: "Where love reigns, there is no will to power; and where the will to power is paramount, love is lacking."*

---

* C. G. Jung, *The Collected Works,* vol. 7, sect. 78 (Princeton: Princeton University Press, 1953).

This antagonistic setup makes one ashamed of the power side of loving (for love exerts a most forceful dominion on whatever it touches); and also Jung's sentence says that to go for power is loveless behavior. They have become mutually exclusive: one or the other.

I think we have in Jung's frank statement the epitome of the romantic view of both love and power. The one all-giving and selfless, the other all-demanding and selfish. The one an expression of soul, the other only of will. And yet we go to workshops to become "empowered"! Perhaps my naming this opposition "romantic" is too confining, since even Machiavelli, the fox of Florence and no romantic, insisted that the soul's domain had nothing to do with the power of princes. Again a distinct separation between an idea of love and an idea of power.

This division leads to the renunciation of power in order to become a nobler, loving soul. Good guys come in last and that's why they are good. Often women are elected or selected because in this opposition they represent soul, not power. So to be disempowered is proof— not of wimpiness and castration necessarily—but of nobility of soul and a loving nature. So, too, idealists and romantics often abjure power. To appropriate power deserts the soul for dirty politics. Is it power that's dirty, or their *idea* of power?

Is this why idealists often lose? So often the question is asked: why do people of nobler intention not try for office in the first place, and when they do get to call the shots and find things going against them, they refuse to find a way through by compromising, but resign, riding off on the high horse of indignation? Why can't the good guys get into the gutter, as was said of Adlai Stevenson?

Even more curious: why are the conflicts about power so ruthless—less so in business and politics, where they are an everyday matter, than in the idealist professions of clergy, medicine, the arts, teaching and nursing. Those embattled in academic struggles and in museum and hospital fights deceive, backbite, threaten and maneuver shamelessly. They will not speak with friends of their enemies. Cabals form. Hatchet men appointed. Revenge plotted. Yet in business and politics competitors for much larger stakes still go off to the golf course, eat and drink together. In business and politics, it seems, there is less idealism and more sense of shadow. Power is not repressed but lived with as a daily companion; moreover, it is not declared to be the enemy of love.

So long as the notion of power is itself corrupted by a romantic opposition with love, soul, goodness and beauty, power will indeed corrupt, as the saying goes. The corruption begins not in power, but in the ignorance about it. That's why we are undertaking these psychological, etymological and philosophical explorations. Giving careful consideration to something, sustaining deep interest in it, isn't this love? Maybe, then, what follows is an exhibition of the love of power.

CONTROL

Perhaps the most common word today associated with power is "control." To be in control. To take control. Yet control derives from an idea that essentially limits power, in fact puts brakes to power like a control switch or the control panel that governs an installation so that it cannot overheat or short-circuit. Control is agency, yes, but of a restrictive kind: the word comes from *contra rotullus,* against the roll.

Since the free flow of inertia follows the path of least resistance, the easy path downhill is controlled by restraints. The complaints to "get the government off our back" and that controlling the military means "fighting with one hand tied" express this hindering sense of control. Control governs more by veto than by leadership, more by checking and balancing a variety of forces than by charging forward like a point man in front of the pack.

When we look closely at what we want when we want to be in control, we find mainly *preventive* desires. We want not to be bugged, not to be demeaned, not to be blocked and criticized. We want obstacles removed that compete, like other divisions in the company and other

gang lords in the 'hood. Control means preventing inter-
ference. It has a conservative effect. So we feel frustrated
by people in control. They won't let us do it our way; they
don't allow freedom; they restrain pleasure; they put all
sorts of comptrollers and paperwork in the way. Why is it,
after all, that so many restrictions and confining rules come
down from the top issued by those in control? And why
that fantasy: "If I were in control here, things wouldn't go
on like this; I wouldn't let things slide; I'd put a stop
to . . ."? Yet when we ourselves get into a position to
"take control," we find that the freedom from restraint we
fought for is restricted by the new restraints we ourselves
have begun to impose. The idea of control controls the
controllers; we are not in control of the power of control.
Still, the fantasy of controlling the roll of the dice or the
wheel of fortune runs deep. It offers power over fate itself.

That great analyst of power, Machiavelli, in his Renaissance classic *The Prince,* conceived of power exactly in
these terms of control versus Fortuna, the capricious Goddess of fate and luck. Machiavelli opposes the two, control
and Fortuna, so that power becomes the ability to control
the unpredictable interventions of Fortuna, those errors,
vices, incompetencies and mess-ups that beset any enterprise. That person who can prevent, direct or inhibit these
eventualities is, in Machiavelli's teachings, a person of
power.

Control as a negative power that inhibits has come
more and more to dominate organizations, both internally

and externally. Internally, by means of meticulous accounting procedures. For instance, the postoperative-care nurse who has to account for wound dressings and not only dress wounds. More memos in triplicate, more requirements to "get back to me on this," more comparative bids, comparative expense items. Externally, by means of security technology—hidden cameras, urine testing, access control, document tracking and shredding, hierarchies and categories of secrecy, tight supervision of computer time, phone calls . . .

When a control freak takes charge, nothing must escape his or her attention—each purchasing order, each expense chit, each "away from the desk." The control freak does not have to manage everything alone to prove that he or she has power. It's not so much "do it my way" as it is "keep me informed." Control means knowing what's going on. Everything must be submitted for inspection. It's the submission that matters. Nothing kept hidden. No locked drawers or closed doors—the open office submits everyone to control.

A more subtle method of control uses loyalty. "Just trust me." "I have to be able to count on you." "You come through for me and I'll cover your back." By bonding loyally to other people, we are bound by them to be at their side and on their side in organizational struggles.

These examples of control—the need to know, to supervise, to check up, to use loyalty as a means—tell us two things. First, they reveal the fact that control weakens power because control constrains its varied expressions. The subterfuge of influence, the manipulations of prestige, the risk of leadership, the silence of resistance do not submit to control and are designed to circumvent it. But these kinds of power are disallowed. Instead of adventuring forward to explore and research unknown territory, control fights a rearguard action, keeping inventory of what has already happened. It likes complete reports. Control, for all its self-assured position of command, relies on a defensive vision, and the traits enumerated—enforced loyalty, exactitude, suspicion of the hidden, watchfulness—are paranoid traits.

So, second, what is the underlying anxiety raised by the idea of losing control? What is really hidden that the paranoia defends against yet never sees? What does "losing control" conjure up? Smashing a window, roaring, screaming, cursing out that bastard boss or that bitch? Bombing the place? A whole range of childish, melodramatic, sloppy, hysterical, crazy behaviors. To be out of control has come to mean wild—and helpless, and thus powerless.

"Out of control" could, however, mean something quite different when we look at these wild fantasies, for they show a vast store of energy let loose. Powerful indeed! Here we begin to uncover another of those mythical infrastructures that govern our feelings and our fears. The mythical figure whose ancient nicknames were "the loosener," "the unbound," "the roarer," and who represented the unstoppable flowing power of natural energy, rather like Freud's pleasure principle, was the God Dionysos. He was celebrated as a child; called God of wetness and drunkenness; ruled the theater and drama; took wild-animal form; and was associated with hysteria and madness.*

Each of the regions of his rule threaten the tightness of control. Wild panther and bull, wet drunk, theatrical bisexual, underworld mystery, vegetative instability, democratic populist, soft child and especially his epithet Lord of the Soul are hardly qualities that belong in the boardroom and the government office. Moreover, Dionysos, who led his followers out of the city and into the woodlands, was never politically correct.

Suppose, however, we shift perspectives. Suppose we try to fathom the power in this configuration from within, rather than trying to keep it under control. What is the essence of Dionysian power? What is the ground of its attraction and endurance through centuries? Control over his power and fear of his excessive effects seem never to work either in the ancient world or in the contemporary psyche. In fact, attempts to control the uncontrollable only exacerbate the excess. Sexual harassment in the correctly

---

* On the nature and attributes of Dionysos, see Walter F. Otto, *Dionysus: Myth and Cult* (Dallas: Spring Publications, 1989), and C. Kerenyi, *Dionysos: Archetypal Image of Indestructible Life* (Princeton: Princeton University Press, 1976); on the Dionysian mysteries and initiation into his kind of power, see Linda Fierz-David, *Women's Dionysian Initiation* (Dallas: Spring Publications, 1988); on the psychology and psychiatry of Dionysos, see Ginette Paris, *Pagan Grace* (Dallas: Spring Publications, 1990), also James Hillman, *The Myth of Analysis* (New York: HarperCollins, 1978), pp. 258–87, with notes.

ordered office exemplifies the exaggerated return of Dionysian vitality in situations of stressed mental despair.

The phrase in our common language that most simply captures the Dionysian mode is: "Go with the flow." Not merely adrift, floating, without compass or port—but flowing with the motions of the psyche. It is like dancing— the Dionysians are depicted usually dancing—where leading and following merge; it is a fusion of one's private consciousness with the field, where borders become imprecise. One develops a special sensitivity to underground reverberations, so that one's will is embraced by the group and represents the group. (Dionysos appears nearly always surrounded by his group, his *thiasos.*) One embodies the consciousness of the group and is ruler (Lord) of its soul by feeling into all that goes on throughout the organization. It comes alive with its own vegetative growth and decay, pulses, seasons. Dionysos was identified with the sap in the vine, the tendrils of the plant, the nourishing milk—the creative juices that are the soul of any system. One cannot control Dionysos, but one can exercise control in a Dionysian fashion by not separating oneself from the unaccountable empowering force that generates all through an organization and is its true bottom line as a vital rhythm. After all, organizations, as the very word declares, are organic, just as corporations, from *corpus,* are living bodies.

It seems rather evident, from an archetypal or mythical perspective, that our ideas about control and the fanatic force we bring to the effort of taking control, staying in control and not letting go of control both in ourselves and in organizations derive from an attempt to master Dionysos. Were we to learn more about his gifts and his ways, gain more insight into the mysteries of his cult and the value of his nature, we might try less for control and actually gain more power.

OFFICE

One sort of power belongs to no one. It is beyond all human power and accrues to a person simply by assuming a position. The power goes with the office. Office can be sharply distinguished from the officeholder's personal ability. American Vice Presidents exemplify the power of office. Spiro Agnew and Dan Quayle, as persons, embodied less than run-of-the-mill political gifts, yet the office of Vice President robed them in the mantle of high agency.

Promotion to higher office increases agency even if you are the same person you were before the elevation. Some, like Harry Truman, another Vice President, rose in stature as they rose in office. But it is the office that gives the person the powers to recognize, appoint, decide and execute. The name on the door, the size of the desk, the view from the window express the invisible power of office made visible by means of trappings. Hence, the crown, the mace, the scepter, the miter, the gavel and Air Force One.

As it comes with office, so it goes with office. The transition at noon on a January 20 when a new President of the United States takes the oath of office most perfectly displays the rising of one citizen to the pinnacle as another, retired from office, departs disempowered into private life. Persons come and go, but the office remains a sanctified residue of impersonal power which the officeholder is obligated not to degrade or vitiate.

Yet office is only a piece of power. In fact, as our examination of the language of power shows, office is merely one phenomenon among many. Without leadership, charisma, authority or influence, a person may well "be in office, but not in power"—to use the damaging phrase Norman Lamont, ex-Chancellor of the Exchequer, shot at his former superior, Prime Minister John Major, before a packed House of Commons.

The word "office" first means service, like the offertory in the Roman Catholic Mass. Post Office is interchangeable with Postal Service. The office in the home, before the Internal Revenue Service revised the definition, once meant the service quarters of a household, the kitchen, pantry, laundry and also outbuildings like barns and privies—the areas of service.

The kind of power that comes with office owes its force to something beyond the job description, the civil service rank, the place in the table of organization, whom you report to and who reports to you. For office suggests an impersonal transcendence that anoints you, as temporary holder of a post that precedes you and continues after your departure, allowing you to provide a service to state, public, church or corporation, that impersonal and indissoluble body which has displaced the earlier kinds of eternal inhuman invisibilities. To hold office is to be in service to something "above" yourself.

In an office you are yourself in service and therefore the Oxford English Dictionary says under the first meaning of the word: "Something done toward anyone; a service, kindness, attention." This is followed by: "Duty towards others; a moral obligation. Duty attaching to one's station, position, or employment . . ." Only the eighth meaning is that of "A place for the transaction of business . . . in which the clerical work of an establishment is done." Sometimes it is difficult to remember the first meanings when seated inside the eighth meaning.

I've come to think that the old "in" basket is the key to performing office work as service. (Productive efficiency wants a piled-high "out" basket, for that has been considered a sign of a generative leadership, while the "in" basket was to be kept light, only essentials pertinent to each particular desk.) Receiving became less and less significant to management, finally to be split off and incarnated in the lowly receptionist, who is paid to screen calls and callers, to look as decorative as the vase of flowers on her desk and to protect management's productive flow into the "out" basket. "Don't call me; I'll call you"—the slogan of the big producer.

That meaning of office as "duty towards others," however, is symbolized by the instruments of reception, from fax to waiting room. We perform service by taking in, hearing the others' requests. Even when one does not act upon what is suggested or comply with what is asked, just giving ear keeps the door open to the sanctum of the office. Becoming, figuratively, your own receptionist shows that "attention and kindness" which defines the original and deepest meaning of office.

PRESTIGE

When the idea of office loses its foundation in service, we are left with office seekers who want the external trappings of office for the power they bestow: prestige. And office seekers are a raging hungry pack. One who didn't get what he wanted shot and killed President Garfield. Others have shot down their former co-workers and bosses, and blown up their places of employment.

Prestige in psychological language is the vanity of narcissism—to be admired and therewith to shore up one's shaky sense of worth. Notice that prestige is not to be worthy of admiration or to earn it, but simply to be assured of personal worth by external approbation given by the office.

Before we judge too sternly, we need to see the communal aspect of this desire for recognition by others. Only the heroic loner, the man with a mission and God's suffering servant can take on tasks without expecting appreciation. Recognition from others is part of communal feedback. In part, we always are as others see us. A great reward of power comes from outside ourselves. Prestige, however, wants only to impress, neither to influence, to dominate, to control, nor to have agency of any sort unless it adds to the impression one makes. In fact, the risks entailed by doing something and failing at it may cost prestige and may keep the person who is intent on prestige from doing much at all. When prestige is the motive, the less you actually do, the more likely success. For you have risked nothing that might detract from your prestige. To maintain prestige, job performance is measured mainly in terms of being present among the important players in important situations.

Is prestige, therefore, an empty substitute for power? Perhaps it does not belong in this discussion at all. Let's look more closely.

A prestigious law firm, a prestigious art gallery or university chair have come to mean places of power, so that power can emanate from prestige as a derivative. First, get into that law firm, have a show at the gallery, be appointed to the chair—and watch your power rise. The ladder of prestige says: join the right clubs, serve on many corporate boards, be seen with the right people, have your name on important contributors' lists. This is the route to power. Note well: these efforts have nothing to do with the straight meaning of power, "the rate at which work is done." In fact, no work may be done at all.

When interviewing someone for promotion or a new opening in management, you may miss something valuable if you judge the candidate using the heroic model. The best candidate may not be the one who wants to turn things around, sweep clean and take charge. Another one, who asks about perks, who his associates will be and the time he can be on his own may be revealing a subversive route to effective power. The manipulation of power through the show of power is also a kind of power. This is the inner secret of prestige.

Again we find that the word gives away this secret. Prestige comes from *praestigia,* delusion, illusion like a juggler's trick, leading to the meanings of deception and imposture. We have the illusion of power without substance; not charismatic magic but manipulation. So to uncover where prestige is ruling, look for juggling, deception, pomp and trappings, a desperate fervor to seize and hold office, and not much real risk. But it's power all the same.

And why? How can power reside in shallow, self-centered caution? How can someone without inner integrity be honored with prestige? Answer: by means of the trappings of office, the role of leadership, the stance of authority—that is, by wearing the mask of power prestige employs the power of the mask.

Early cave paintings, aboriginal facial markings, Greek and Japanese drama each show that the mask retains and emanates effective agency. Surrounding the hollow personality of the prestige-driven person lies the archetypal aura of the mask. By means of the mask something more than human is present, a higher drama is being played and greater powers are being invoked. These powers come through the stance and voice and advice of its wearer, enlarging his stature and bestowing importance. Inside this persona there may be no one at home, or only a weak comedian playing the Wizard of Oz; even if seen into and seen through, the person retains a position of power acquired only by prestige.

Again, why? What is the juggler's trick? The main method for acquiring prestige is not the imitation of leadership or authority, but rather having a keen nose for what and who is important. Someone with prestige gathers followers simply by following what's in the wind, which way it blows, when to trim sails, shift weight, reverse course, take cover. Since they are inwardly empty, they are utterly under the influence of outer forces. Therefore they can sense immediately the matter of importance in the air. His conversation will drop names; hers will remark on events others missed. All along they will indicate how well "up" on things they are and where the "major moves" are taking place.

The condemnation of prestige as false reputation goes back a long way. Cicero *(De Officiis)* refers to a supposed remark of Socrates: "Make yourself the sort of man you want people to think you are" (Xenophon, *Memorabilia* II). This advice opens the door wide for prestige, for the sentence can be understood to mean: seek reputation by playing the role, putting on the mask. And so Cicero warns —rather uselessly, I believe—that it is a "serious misapprehension" that any "permanent reputation can be won by pretense, or empty display, or hypocritical talk, or by putting on an insincere facial expression . . ." Even the ancient wise men could miss the ball, because is it not precisely by these manipulative means that prestige does gain reputation? Below the seeming and the deception, however, is a transcendental awareness of importance.

EXHIBITIONISM

Because prestige shows off, psychoanalysts are tempted to see in it the sexual pleasures of exhibitionism. Abnormal psychology defines exhibitionism as "an inappropriate and/or compulsive display of the genitals." A secondary meaning is "exaggerated efforts to call attention to oneself." This second, widened meaning suggests that the person as a whole becomes genitalized, like the rock stars from Elvis through Mick Jagger to Madonna (or in reverse, degenitalized like Michael Jackson), and therewith fascinating.

One can hold power by "exaggerated efforts to call attention to oneself," taking any opportunity to show off what you have just accomplished—celebrations, memos, press releases, special meetings. What will he think of next! Did you see what she was wearing at the convention banquet! Fascinating!

Although abnormal psychology may label showing off as "inappropriate," "compulsive" and "exaggerated," an archetypal psychology considers the sexual aura of fascinating display to belong authentically to power. *Fascinum* was a standard Roman name for representations of the penis. A *fascinum* referred mainly to an apotropaic charm in the shape of genitals used to ward off evil and bad luck. The lewd gestures in the pop arena may be disclosing more than the personal compulsions of the star on stage. They also may be exhibitions of the power of sex to ward off the evils of prurient repression that would deny genital power to the body politic. Hypocrisy, censorship and "cool" hide our flesh in the button-down collar and button-up lip of corporate correctness.

If you can't take the heat, stay out of the kitchen— that White House slogan for the ability to absorb the pressures of power may be transposed to say: if you can't flaunt sexual enjoyment, get out of the limelight.

Any position of power—office, leadership, authority, prestige—emits the vibrations of high potency: pay attention, I am a potent person; I hold down a big job. If the show of potency belongs to power, then one way to claim power may take the route of genitalized behavior. This may account for some of the sexual harassment that goes on in the workplace. The exhibition of sexuality also belongs to the power scene, the power structure, the power atmosphere in the contemporary workplace, especially when power is defined by the repressive meaning of control.

Here, we must make a very important distinction. Exhibitionism should not be given only a genital meaning. Sexual display is only one specific form of general animal display. Even more fundamental to animal life than sexual exhibition—which in "higher" animals is seasonal and therefore infrequent—is display itself. Even the simplest oceanic creatures display their natures; and from the staggering, helpless beginning of life among mammals, their colorings and shapes, their coats and cries display their kind. Life shows off, from the very beginning.

By "display" I do not mean only the elaborate exhibitions animals put on to lure, to threaten, to protect and to mark territory. According to the eminent Swiss biologist and philosopher of nature Adolf Portmann, self-presentation *(Selbst-Darstellung)* for animal life is as primary as self-preservation. Because we have learned to think of animals within a competitive capitalist framework of scarcity and predation, we look at what they do only functionally. Portmann disagrees. He insists that display is not reducible to any single function and is, for instance, narrowly sexual only in particular circumstances. Each species shows off its style without any purpose other than to show itself (as some birdsong), to manifest its essential capacity, and perhaps for its own pleasure. For us human animals this implies that exhibitionism is not only a sexual act but a display of one's innate nature. It displays one's power: how you come on shows who you are.

Perhaps that's how Adam at the beginning of the Bible knew each animal's name. They showed him who they were by their strut and gait, their stripes and scales, flaunting their elaborate heads and facial markings at one end and their patterned, tail-swishing, aromatic rears at the other. Here I am, they said to Adam, look me all over; see my kind of power which gives me my name.

We human animals also are compelled to display ourselves, if not directly by frontal exposure, then by clothes, office decor, hairstyle, stationery, kind of car, gestures, manners, speech, perfume, nails, shoes—and by personal achievements. See my kind of power which gives me my name. No matter how carefully sublimated, power shows, and shows itself off. It seems to take pleasure in itself and give pleasure to those who have it. Showing off as turning on. But the turn-on is not, I repeat, the root of the showing off. Display of a wider basic kind runs deep in our animal natures.

Again we have to make a distinction. For not all power is compelled to show itself. We have to distinguish between the exhibition of power on the one hand and covert operations of power on the other. Power brokers behind the scenes; the old ward heelers in cigar-smoky rooms carving up the territory; the nameless dealers in weapons, cocaine and foreign policy. Exhibition is not cloakroom power, paranoid power, golf-course power, cover-up power. Exhibition is the blatant generous showmanship of codpiece and cleavage and bustle that plumps the behind. With this power comes high fashion and flash, that elegance which always went along with pirates and buccaneers, warlords, boxers and big-time gamblers, divas, society hostesses and queens. It's the exhibitionism of palaces and city-block brownstone mansions, long limos, liveried servants and bodyguards. I am who I am and you know who I am because you can see who I am—and it's exciting. It attracts not because it's sexy; it's sexy because it displays power that can protect against bad luck. Maybe all that lingers of personal exhibitionistic protest are concealed suspenders and daring socks or secretly Victorian camisoles. The hip silicon style of new niche companies where personal nonchalance is de rigueur confirms in reverse my point. Whether tight and stiff or bright, loose and easy, an organization has a form, and part of its control over its members is the influencing of the style of their display.

The current convention of sexless behavior in the workplace—or is it not new, merely the same old heroic puritanism making its cyclical return?—insists that the erotics of power must be utterly suppressed from places of power like Senate offices, officers' messes and executive clubs. This suppression confuses the power of sexual exhibition with the power of sexual harassment—bugging those below you with genital intentions and for genital favors. But actual diagnosed exhibitionists do not ask for follow-through. They do not harass their victims for genital favors. All they say is "look at me." Flash and gone.

Suppose we now were to imagine that the repression of the natural animal display of one's power, by bureaucratic and legalistic correctness, rather than eliminating sexual harassment may foster it. If self-display, which necessarily has an erotic aura to it, becomes immediately translated as self-exposure, how can one show off with Big Brother watching? He watches—not as a fascinated voyeur, but as the gray ghost of a governor of the Massachusetts Bay Colony, that haunting American puritan who can never be laid to rest. Maybe voyeurism (the joy of looking equivalent to the joy of showing) and thinking pagan thoughts and the compelling pressures that build under the formalities of offices are one side of the same coin on whose reverse face is that governing ghost. If the display of power is reduced to sexual exhibitionism, we will all be buying sturdy clothes from L. L. Bean, which does a stalwart job of eliminating any erotic innuendo. But censorship and correctness will not work, because as Freud said long ago, the repressed always returns and the drive to display will harass us with ever more directly sexual demands. For two reasons: first, because some kinds of power like to show off; and second, the sexual, though not the basis of the display of power, is nevertheless basic to the fascination of power.

AMBITION

The desire to hold office, to gain power in any form, often suffers condemnation, even if recruiters look for ambitious young graduates who want to climb the ladder. Ambition has been defined, snidely, as "reach exceeding grasp" and "aspiration beyond competence." Or as hubris (excess of pride), perhaps the worst of all Greek faults of character. Vaulting pride in one's own capacity; no need of the Gods; no need of the counsel of mentors—this is the ambition universally condemned in tragic literature and heroic epic. Cocaine, uppers and muscle-building steroids are the concrete examples in our world of ambitious hubris. They show that enhanced performance follows a truly mythical pattern—an extraordinary rise and a disastrous fall. The one single wisdom taught by all the classical stories is: remember the limits put on mortals by the immortals (as the Greeks called their divinities).

A traditional West African song advises:

Do not seek too much fame,

but do not seek obscurity.

Be proud.

But do not remind the world of your deeds.

> Excel when you must,
> but do not excel the world.
> Many heroes are not yet born.
> many have already died.
> To be alive to hear this song is a victory.*

This practical wisdom warns against trying for heaven—it leads only to hell. Keep to the limits of the actual world. Staying alive proudly is ambition enough.

However, when we search the word, "ambition" reveals some pleasing features. Ambit means circuit, circumference, compass. Ambition as full compass, all around, the whole hog. *Ambire* in Rome designated the going-around of a candidate for office, canvassing for votes, which leads to the second meaning of soliciting, fawning, so that an ambitious person can be narrowly described as one seeking office. But more widely, the going-around fills out the ambit and paces out step by step (ambulation) the dimensions of one's personal kingdom, measuring one's size. Ambition takes one to the edges of one's limits, to the "verge" as the dictionary says.

The ambitious are said to have an "appetite" for power. Mighty figures in myth like the Norse giants and the Greek Titans, and the huge creatures in fairy tales and Disney cartoons, as well as the immense eater Gargantua in the French tale by Rabelais, all have humongous appetites. They want everything in the world. The common notion of

---

* "Old Song" in *The Rag and Bone Shop of the Heart,* R. Bly, J. Hillman and M. Meade, eds. (New York: HarperCollins, 1992), p. 498.

appetite has become reduced to general drives like hunger and thirst, so that the word constellates fears of putting on weight and drinking too much. The basic idea of appetite, however, shows that the reach and aspiration of ambition are located in the word "appetite," which comes from *petere,* the Latin translation of the Greek word *orexis* (our *anorexia*: without appetite). *Orexis* means desire, yearning, craving; its root, *oregein,* means to reach out with the hand, to stretch the fingers to grasp.

If we go deeper, we find something stranger still: *petere,* and therefore appetite, is cognate with *ptero,* the Greek for the wing of a bird, and the structure of that wing is homologous with our human fingers. Etymology says we fly with the imagination in our hands by means of our making and doing (the first definition of power as agency). The appetite in ambition lifts us off the ground and carries us to that verge of the farthest possibility. Perhaps, then, the attempts to control the appetite by diet are scientistic, unimaginative means of reducing the wings of desire and the power of ambition to the properly correct proportions of the puritan corset. I am saying that appetite control is an unconscious substitute for the control of ambition. The fear of flying.

So ambition in the truest sense of the term calls for risk—going for it! No one can know beforehand how wide the perimeter, how far the ambition will carry until you've gone too far and are declared to be overambitious. It is this risking extremes that makes us condemn ambition in people and yet often praise it in a work of art or political program. An ambitious intention aspires; it sets itself high goals and takes the necessary risks. Circumstances, other people, the recalcitrance of things and the Goddess Fortuna set the limits on ambition. We pretend it is a fatal flaw in character, that one did not calculate right, could have foreseen what was coming. These cautions after the fact locate ambition wholly within a person as if it were a trait to be controlled, whereas the term that is crucial here is the vaulting nature of ambition to go to the verge. At the other side of the edge and beyond it is the wholly unforeseeable, and ambition seeks by its very nature to go too far. Self-limitation, by means of willpower and developed self-control as a braking restraint, misses the inner sense of ambition which must go beyond better judgment, risking the impossible. To exceed, risk excess. As William Blake the poet said, in his *Proverbs from Hell:* "You never know what is enough unless you know what is more than enough," and "The road of excess leads to the palace of wisdom."

REPUTATION

John Adams, the second American President, a capable though somewhat modest and stubborn man, admitted to a "passion for distinction." That's what drove him. He had an ambition to be recognized. In more contemporary language, the "passion for distinction" becomes fame. *Fame Is the Spur,* as a novel of some years ago was called; fame, if even only for fifteen minutes, as Andy Warhol said.

Fame has a rich and famous career. The Roman idea of *fama* meant first of all "the talk of the multitude," what the people are saying in their rumors and gossip, the traditional sayings about a person, place or subject. A second derived meaning of *fama* is public opinion as a more objective guide to the character of a person, which, if good, becomes renown, and if bad, infamous and disreputable. Behind the vagaries of fame, behind the rise and fall in public opinion, was the figure of a Goddess, Fama, fame personified, "swift-footed, all-seeing, growing as she runs." And, as described by Virgil, she runs with a terrible speed, becoming monstrous in size, increasing especially at night, and her body is covered with feathers as well as with countless eyes, tongues, mouths and ears—the equipment of rumor.

Fama became "reputation" in the Renaissance when it played a major role in the psychology of motivation. In those amazing figures of Renaissance Italy and the similarly amazing characters in Shakespeare, we find that *fama*/reputation was an overriding concern. They insisted that reputation must always be considered—its extension through deeds of honor, its protection against calumny. One must never forget the ruin incurred if a reputation was blemished, a ruin not only to one's career but to one's associates, party, family, friends and city.

Especially the city, by which is meant the common good, whether it be the land and its people, a bank, or a public institution like the law courts and a university, or a major corporation like Johnson & Johnson or R. J. Reynolds. In Shakespeare's *Richard II* (II, i, 50ff.), old Gaunt in a famous speech eulogizes England: "This blessed plot, this earth, this realm . . . This land of such dear souls, this dear, dear land, / Dear for her reputation through the world." The power of the land is so tied with its reputation that if its reputation falls so does its power.

Four hundred years later Shakespeare's high style for kings and queens becomes the overblown hype of image fixers, the adman's spin to protect your image, the image of the President, of the nation. How are we perceived; what do the polls say? Immense sums and smart brains are put to work to keep the image polished. A sullied reputation downgrades even your credit rating.

A more personal and poignant example comes from Shakespeare's *Othello* (II, iii, 262). Othello's lieutenant, the "good," "true" and "valiant" Cassio (who falls prey to the manipulations of Iago), in his worst moment exclaims: "Reputation, reputation, reputation! O, I have lost my reputation! I have lost the immortal part of myself, and what remains is bestial. My reputation, Iago, my reputation!"

Cassio's speech gives a clue for better grasping what John Adams wanted with his "passion for distinction." Reputation refers to the immortal part of the soul which seeks to rise from obscurity to visibility in the eyes of the world. Lowly beginnings in poverty, an oppressed and abused childhood, ignominy in the crowd, according to the idea spoken by Cassio, keeps the soul in the bestial world. "Bestial" here means simply unenlightened, caught in the turmoils of instinctual habits, unredeemed by the angel. The reputation of a person affects that person's angel, the part of a person that is born with us, accompanies us through life, though remaining invisible. It is the angel that is elevated or sullied by our actions and rises or falls with the alterations of our *fama*. Cassio cries out for the loss of his angel and the consequential possibility of the loss of his soul. If the angel falls, the soul may have lost its chance at redemption. So we see that the drive to fame and the concern with reputation—if but adding another measly item to your résumé—derive from deep spiritual springs. Because reputation means redemption from a low life, then the passion for distinction is a call of the angel who would be lifted into light, even if limelight.

What I am calling the "angel" that was born with us and is our secret companion, Socrates called his *daimon,* who guarded him from wrong moves. The same figure appears in German thought as the *Doppelgänger* and in ancient thought as the *genius.* Our birthday celebrations with cake and candles originate in a ritual honoring, not you, but your genius who was born with you. *You* are never a genius, can never be a genius, but you are guided and protected by a genius, and your life must be led so that the genius is not damaged. Damage to it through wounded reputation (and Cassio uses the language of wounding as Gaunt uses the language of shame) reflects especially on the family, for one's genius derives partly from the family and is generated in the family marriage bed *(lectus genialis).* Your genius or angel is conceived with you, descends into you through your generators and is like an invisible twin at birth, part of your psychic inheritance.

In today's language, damage to your image affects not only you. It affects your followers, partisans, apprentices— what once were your descendants and household. Damage to your image also affects your protectors, mentors, promoters, those backers behind you who once were called your guardian ancestors. Each individual person as the focus of all these forces stands as a pillar of power, striving to keep his or her image intact by alignment with the inner angel. "To thine own self be true," advises the old man whom Hamlet kills in an ironic show of how Hamlet is true to his own kind of madness. This "true self" is how we today speak of the angel. By locating this true self, this angel, inside our private person, inside even our skin, we regard our external image and its reputation as merely a mask, or what psychology calls a persona. The persona, says psychology, is definitely not the true self. That mask is only a mode of adapting to the institutions of society, only a role and not the true inner "me."

This personal and private way of thinking about one's image divides what we do in the world from what we believe we really are inside, and so we forget that the supposedly superficial image of the persona is the exterior face of the self that is actually and truly you. The husk and the shell belong as much to the complete nut as does the kernel. And the value of the nut is given by the desires of society for it. A good nut has a good reputation. At least some of its value depends on popular opinion. All by itself, sweet as the kernel may be, it will hang on the tree and wither. "To be is to be perceived," wrote the philosopher Berkeley. To denigrate the face society perceives, to feel above one's reputation and "what they are saying" betrays a contempt for both the judgment of others and for the angel who lives as much in your actions with others as in your opinion of yourself. That belief which insists the angel lives only in the kernel makes it so very difficult to "see ourselves as others see us."

Popular opinion may be manipulated, spin doctors may skew the images, the true self reduced to a sound bite —nonetheless, what the polls say and the value of your true self belong together, just as what your family thinks of you and what you think of yourself are not as distant as our delusional grandeur of independence would have us believe. Your genius is also theirs. Your angel isn't only yours to have and to hold. The apple doesn't fall that far from the tree.

So the victors say, "Hello, Mom," and wave to Pop on TV after an Olympic triumph; so they thank the family and bring them onstage on election night's celebration party; so they say, "All I am I owe to my family." Not the family as such, but the genius, the guiding angel that gives the passion for distinction and pushes a person from being buried in the bestial darkness of obscurity into the limelight. Redeemed, if only for fifteen minutes.

INFLUENCE

On the one hand, influence can flow into the life of others, fecundating, inseminating an organization without direct subordination of others. On the other hand, influence can mean surreptitiously infiltrating into others by means of propaganda, punishment and rewards, and manipulations. In both cases of this good-bad division, influence is imagined as activity. You come under my influence; I have influence in high places; I'm grateful to you for having influenced my career in the right direction.

Another idea of influence is far less active. We can be influential simply by holding fast to a position, to principles, to a way of being that everything around must take into account. No longer is it a question whether your influence is good or bad, but rather a matter of influencing all events simply by your presence as things flow around, through and by you. It is like a rock in a riverbed. The rock does not move, yet it influences the course of the river. The river must take it into account—go around it, over it, speed up, slow down, because of the stubborn presence of the stone. The stone doesn't manipulate the river, or convince it to share its ideology. It has no control over what happens. It merely says: I'm here, too.

Perhaps this is a useful way to read the stubborn defensive clinging to office of those who will not resign, even after losing battles. If I imagine myself a stone in the riverbed, I will always be run over, but not washed away. I will always go down in defeat before the rush of events and be subordinated to superior active forces. But when the flood is over and a dry season comes, I'm still there, more than ever. I cling to my turf, I am my territory. I shall not give up my office since I am resigned by nature to the fact that my power resides in sinking deeper into the rock bottom of my place. Only by continually deepening (not by adapting) and by making weightier my position can my influence in the geography as a whole be affirmed.

A more inspired notion of influence comes from Henry Adams (1838–1918), the distinguished American elder who said that "susceptibility to the highest forces is the highest genius." Here, the power of influence turns altogether away from my effect on you or yours on me. Here, influence means suggestibility, the capacity to receive these "highest forces." But what and who are they? Members of the board, senators, lobbyists with caches of cash? Or are they perhaps the writings of ancient philosophers and the visitations of informative dreams?

To be open to influence of the sort Adams recommends requires, first, to be clear about what you consider to be "the highest forces" and, second, to refine your

susceptibility so that you can filter all the information coming in. The old theologians called this filtering *diakrisis,*
discerning the spirits. Without discernment, they thought
you could become a dupe of the devil. Discernment allows
you to be more sophisticated about the forces, hearing
them metaphorically and not only literally, so that you do
not become a mouthpiece of your mentor or a channel of
visionary wisdom masking as genius.

RESISTANCE

The idea of influence that we just sketched flows easily into another kind of power, the power to resist. Without resistance, subordination makes no sense. There is nothing there to put down. Willpower must bump up against something, push something or someone around. The simplest idea of power supposes that for work to be done, there be something that resists. Overcoming resistance and lowering resistance are important notions in thinking about heat, electricity and also psychoanalysis. It seems that resistance, as the contrary to the exertion of power, makes power possible. We already saw this idea in regard to control, from *contra rotullus,* against the roll of inertia. Power, without the resistance of a counterforce, mimics the inertia it strives against, becoming an unhindered, tensionless expansion, following the lay of the land, flattening out into stagnant accumulations without intention, much like the pictures we make of inert despots on fat pillows in their pleasure domes, all resistance to these plenipotentiaries overcome.

Hence revolutions do not aspire really to utopia but instead call for perpetual revolution, a continuing struggle between revolutionaries and counterrevolutionaries, the stubborn pockets of resistance that keep the revolution alive.

Moreover, resistance seems built into the universe as part of its wiring. Each and every thing seems to want to remain where it is and exactly how it is, for that is what it is. Once this was called the formal cause, the essential nature, that gives each and every thing its internal power to exist. The world seems to like the status quo; it resists change despite what mystics say about change being the only truth and what nuclear physicists say about the motion of waves and particles as the fluctuating instability inside all solid substance. According to the philosopher Spinoza, substance wills itself to persist; resistance is built into its nature. According to the philosopher Bergson, for anything to exist at all it must endure through time. It must in some way stay the same. Sameness is one of the great categories of existence. Look at your own life for evidence. On the one hand, you can recognize all the changes and differences from ten years ago; on the other, you can feel that your personality, your nature, your ways are just as they always were. New job, new ideas, new city—everything different; but meet your father or a former spouse and you are right where you always were—everything the same.

What power it takes to move one habit—as AA recovery groups have shown; just as it takes power to move one shovelful of dirt from here to there. Little wonder that power can be most simply defined in terms of work done.

Work is so hard, the power required so great because of the resistance factor. And that is why changes are so difficult to achieve and so miraculous when they do occur. And also why quick change is suspicious, for unless the pattern of resistance itself has been altered, the change remains whitewash and wallpaper. The underlying stone walls remain stuck in their stasis and want to stay that way.

Essentially, perhaps managing anything—a task, a person, one's own life—means dealing with its inherent resistance, and we employ whatever means of power we can: influence, tyranny, persuasion, fear, control. The manager has to work against the resistance of the staff, the obduracy of problems that won't go away, the sales force that sticks to its forms and finally buyers' resistance to the product itself. To say nothing of his own inertia. There is resistance all down the line. Something in every system wants to remain the same.

When we defend our own turf, become stubborn as mules rather than comply with new regulations, something larger is going on in the pattern as a whole than merely my personal obstinacy. Easy accommodation to the rules may look to be the smoother course for the system as a whole. To believe, however, that a system works best when it works smoothest is a simplistic model, like the childish model of an ideal parent who gives no trouble. Power wants trouble; power as the play of forces enjoys the reluctant complexes that will not submit, the team member who won't just adapt, the disobedient son who challenges decisions. These components of any system serve the power of the whole, keeping it in a state of high tension. In any system, whether a corporation, a family or the inner arrangements of the human psyche, a vigorous "no" to the good of the whole may serve the good of the whole and increase its power even more than a compliant "yes."

LEADERSHIP

Descriptions of leadership take metaphors and models from animals. The best-known of these is the "alpha animal," that big buck who leads the herd by virtue of its innate wiliness, its size and strength. This leader, as some barnyards and university labs show, need not be a male animal. Hens can kill roosters. This alpha-animal model relies on a domination notion of power; it neglects the fact that there are a dozen ways of "leading" illustrated by female animals: the young moose cow dances to gain the bull's attention and entry to his group; the female crocodile selects her mate by refusing the advances of others; lionesses hunt together and make the kill; cows can lead the herd to summer pasture on alpine slopes. So to begin, let's free the idea of leadership from images of the biggest, the bravest and the brawniest.

Yet, from watching TV nature shows, we do tend to associate leaders with the first vulture at the carnage, the large wolf that puts down younger male challengers. Under the spell of images we forget that we are watching more than animals; we are being scripted into a particular narrative that may fit the economic philosophy of humans who back the show more than the animals being shown. From Aesop's fables to Disney's cartoons, animals easily become exemplars of human ideas, and the message transmitted by nature shows may be closer to the kind of 1980s "nature" exhibited on *Falcon Crest* and *Dallas* than the actual law of the jungle or the call of the wild.

From these TV animals we distill an idea of leadership: power as predation, competition, ever-present danger (paranoia), sexual domination and possession, threat and warning, tension and stress, survival of the fittest in a hostile environment, scarcity. Without the narration, we might "hear" another tale being told: of cooperation, of restraint, of play and adaptation and even of pleasure and beauty. And we see leadership as being in harmony with and *following* the innate will of the group rather than trying to dominate the group.

A culture sees in animals its own myths. This idea is transparent enough when Eurocentric anthropologists report Australian and African tribal beliefs. It is far more difficult to see myths in our own reports on animal behavior that we call scientific observation. We believe we are seeing facts, but the arrangement of the facts reveals ideas, and the facts and ideas are together compiled along mythical grids which are especially powerful when we observe anything that cannot talk back to us in our terms, such as little babies, foreign peoples, the insane and retarded and animals. Yet how many ideas about the "true nature" of human beings are drawn from just these fields of wild surmise. Next time a nature show comes on TV, try turning off the sound and observe what ideas the parade of images evokes in your mind.

After that strong disclaimer, which should invalidate what I am about to say in this paragraph, I, too, want to use animal metaphors for suggesting an idea of leadership as a natural unlearned power: the "born leader." Some horses on the track will not let another horse pass it. Trail horses have to file out in a specific order or else some will always hold back to follow and others will always be nipping at the tail of the horse in front. Some kittens, even if smaller at first, soon push to the nipple before the rest. They prove more curious, adventuresome—or have a more urgent appetite. The leader cannot help but come forward and cannot help being pushed forward by others who intuitively recognize leadership and submit to a hierarchical structure, the pecking order.

The animal serves especially well for putting over that quality of leadership which unites thought and action in a single gesture. My notion of animal intelligence imagines it as a kind of behavior rather than as a kind of reflection. I imagine that animals do not suffer the fault of Hamlet, in whom the will's "resolution / Is sicklied o'er with the pale cast of thought." Like Hamlet, we civilized humans suffer the split of thought and action—thoughtless actions regretted afterward, and the paralysis of action in which all agency wastes away in deliberation of a deed that never comes to pass.

Management's rational planning cycle moves back and forth from engagement to reflection to reengagement, and so on. We are taught that we learn from mistakes in action, the trial-and-error system of developmental improvement. Even depth psychology accepts this idea of separation between thought and action. We bring our actions of yesterday to the therapist's office for reflection, and we reflect in advance about the actions of tomorrow.

The French have an accurate phrase that captures in an image the unpleasant feelings of this split: *l'esprit de l'escalier,* the spirit of the staircase, the moment after leaving the room and going down the stairs, when it comes to your mind—too late—what you could have done, should have said, would do if you had another chance. Thought following action out of sync. Victorian English called it "afterwit." The whole aim of life could be nothing more than overcoming this Hamletian disjunction on the model of the Zen master or the animal.

The squirrel leaps, the cat pounces, the hawk soars and hovers and then plummets into its dive, the situation affording to the animal's senses the exact information it needs for an instantaneity of thought and action. Less reflection than reflex. The animal sense in the leader reads the situation with the intense concentrated noticing of the cat and the hawk.

Leadership, therefore, may well require something more than the usual qualities of determination, the capacity to listen to all sides and coordinate among them, and the courage of risk behavior, as well as all the moral virtues we can learn from the Boy Scout handbook and the management textbook. Nothing wrong at all with these qualities. But the essence of leadership may lie more in the capacity to overcome in one stroke the ghost of Hamlet, who is the spirit of the staircase. And the leader's power would reside in a behaved intelligence, defined as an exquisitely fine-tuned attention linked immediately with a reflexive response. Thus anyone aspiring to leadership may learn more on the basketball court or while fly-fishing than in business school, since the great task is to approximate ever more and more closely the two powers that our Hamletian culture, with its wounded "inner animal" (rather than abused "inner child"), continues to separate: thought and action.

Supposedly, the most sublime action is reflection upon action. This is the instruction of Taoism, of the Hindu *Bhagavad-Gita,* of Jesus' sermons and St. Paul's letters. Reflection before or after action is also what goes on in psychotherapy. So my model which unites the two in a single reflexive moment is heretical to a good deal of traditional teaching. This model is also dangerous, for the sudden animal act that claims to be a sure and true reflex may merely mask unrefined impulse justifying itself as instinct. Not everything one does suddenly and without forethought is therefore like the squirrel jumping to another branch. The squirrel takes in the entire environmental situation. She may not seem to look before she leaps, but she surely looks and leaps simultaneously. Unpremeditated action may be a hallmark of the leader, but it can cut two ways. Beatings, rapes, bar fights, suicides and murders are sometimes as spontaneous as the dive into the icy pond to save a child's life.

The mystery of leadership may have little to do with heroics, ambition, influence or even authority derived from wide recognition by others for your competence and judgment. You may have authority yet not be a leader, and the term "hidden leader" shows this distinction. The hidden leader in an organization or at a meeting neither sets the agenda, forces the decisions, nor executes the program. The hidden leader is not in charge, even though his or her authority tilts the discussion throughout in a distinct direction.

The single most valuable characteristic of the hidden leader is again an animal trait. He or she remains hidden, like a moray eel, watching and waiting for the right moment, *kairos,* as the Greeks called the opportune instant. According to Machiavelli, there is only one propitious moment, the *occasione,* when the complex causes of Fate and Fortune can be managed by the leader. This capacity to recognize the *occasione* is crucial to the exercise of leadership and grants it power over circumstances. At any meeting, it is the timing of an intervention that turns the tide. Not only does the hidden leader hide his hand; he also anticipates what's in the wind, has a sense for the invisible, the hidden, which the president and the chairperson, occupied with their agendas and their positions, cannot perceive. The big buck antelope sparks the herd a fraction of a second before the others notice. He's tuned to the hidden.

Since we are claiming that leaders are born and not made, they may come to the fore without having been tested. They may wear no medals, have no awards on the wall. He or she may have never won the blue ribbon. Fairy tales of the dumb one, the little tailor, the lamed soldier, handless maiden or the third weak sister and abandoned child, as well as those old movies of hesitant Jimmy Stewart, sensitive Henry Fonda and laconic, shy Gary Cooper, reveal (in their stories and films) leaders who can be modest, awkward, uncertain, retiring, even afraid. Yet they come to the fore when the situation demands. Like an inborn release mechanism in animals, leadership is called forth by circumstances. The person rises to the occasion and the group falls in behind. He or she solves the enigma, resolving the crisis for the community. The man alone on horseback and the clever princess in her tower are not leaders, since they have no community and serve no followers.

This idea of leadership may be the secret prompter that fires ambition, demands office and resists accommodation. It's in the nature of the horse and the kitten, and it will out. If this animal impetus is not allowed, if no circumstance is offered by the environment, the frustrated drive diverts into secondary gains. We attempt substitutes, the pseudo-leadership of prestige, fearsomeness or a haughty purism that is "too good to step forward." For some the opportunity to lead may come too late or not at all and this missed necessity to fulfill an animal function may cause more pain in older age than all past failures and misdemeanors.

Despite my reliance on animal metaphors for describing the nature of leadership, let's not forget that leaders are the embodiment of ideas. Neither the blessing, or curse, of charisma nor the instinctual surety of decisiveness assures a leader of the following necessary for effective accomplishment. What ultimately gives one the power of leadership is a capacity to embody visionary ideas, to be unafraid of ideals. Strong personality traits are given to many, but the representation and expression of ideals is given to few. It is precisely here that the idea of leadership transcends its animal base in reflex action and affirms a second spiritual base in the psyche's need to idealize, to imagine the far-off and the wonderful and let itself be captivated by vision. Idealism is itself an immense power mobilizing whole peoples, whole continents, and when present in a living figure like Simón Bolívar, like Lenin, leadership becomes the instrument of history.

CONCENTRATION

We begin by looking at old movies for images of concentrated power: the oak-paneled library set where the evil widow now owns all the stock in the company; the somber magnate alone in his Western railroad car; the tight-lipped Mafia boss under his black hat, back to the restaurant wall; the kung fu teacher utterly focused, utterly compact; the paranoid enemy of James Bond, isolated and impregnable, the concentric focus of a world empire; the frail churchgoing schoolteacher whose single-minded determination turns the frontier around. Or imagine Rodin's statue of *The Thinker*—that head, that fist, that concentration. Images of power.

In the textbooks of business today, concentration of power gets poor marks. A chief executive, a board or a company are considered to be on the wrong managerial road when power is concentrated in too few hands. Power is to be decentralized among subsets, each with its own decision-making and profit-generating autonomy. Centers of power are to be loosened, empowerment shared. Cooperatives, teams, worker-shareholders, conversations rather than directives, networks.

The network replaces the turbine as a governing image. Today, not the massive dynamo of tightly coiled wires wrapped around themselves, not even the tightly packed silicon wafer; but the images of flow, feedback, distributive energy, touching all the bases, balancing constituencies, delivery—an indeterminate field of almost random forces —are the new images of power. Not the heart, the capillaries.

The famous lines of the greatest of Irish poets, William Butler Yeats, which prophesied the horrors of Western civilization during the first part of the twentieth century—"Things fall apart; the centre cannot hold; / Mere anarchy is loosed upon the world"—also foreshadowed the chaos and catastrophe theories of the latter part of the century, theories which void the center in favor of creative innovation, freeing enterprise to find its niche and do its thing any which way it can. The center *should* not hold so that things may indeed fall apart. All you need is access with the help of compatibilities. The internet linkup is where power resides.

Power comes in to any of us by being plugged in—or rather, power *is* being plugged in, since there is no single generative source. The concentration which "Think" requires, like the corporation whose motto it was, gradually gives way to Stay-in-Touch.

Despite these trends, concentration remains a distinct proclivity of the human mind. Something about the mind enjoys a focused immersion into itself. To bring careful consideration to a single question, to evaluate options and set priorities, to lay out an intelligent schedule, to listen without distraction, to observe, attend, analyze, mull—all this calls for a power of mind beyond the "takes" of aides and the briefings of experts. Hercule Poirot in the Agatha Christie detective novels called this capacity his "little grey cells," by which he meant not mere "smarts" but the ability to concentrate fully on the puzzles of the crime, its circumstances, the characters, motives, alibis. All held together in the intensity of thought, resulting in masterful strokes of action.

The idea has occurred to me of a possible relation between lack of concentration in schoolchildren, which psychiatry calls "attention deficit disorder," and the increased violence with weapons in the same population. The intense concentrated power of a weapon—gun, knife, club, chain—may offer single-minded focus to a distractible and diffuse consciousness that surfs through the day as if it, too, were part of the media, all channels on at once. If, as I am suggesting, the psyche desires to concentrate, then a weapon may be satisfying what the schoolroom does not afford. Besides policing weapons, we might search for methods of teaching that capture attention and evoke concentration—images, dramas, rituals, rhythms—thereby transferring power back from the weapon to the child's mind.

My emphasis on concentration as power, and a power that the psyche needs and enjoys, takes us away from current ideas of leadership as learning—that is, the idea that the power of an advanced leader lies mainly in an ability to stay open. The very word "concentration" means closed circles, self-enclosure, inward focus, density, intensity. Surely, it will be said, such a mind will asphyxiate in its own closet, breathing only its own exhalations. No winds of change blowing through, no assimilation of new input, and so it cannot learn and therefore cannot lead. From this standpoint, concentration looks like withdrawal and the abdication of power.

However, concentration finds its learning elsewhere and receives input from other sources rather than other people. This is the introverted style of power found in the shaman, the recluse, the hermit, the mystic, the contemplative. They turn to dreams, meditations, reveries, signs, omens, old texts, motions of nature and "sessions of sweet silent thought." Concentration gives access to other powers—inner, hidden and highly suspect to the everyday camaraderie of business. It attempts connection with genius, with inspiration. It trusts solitude. It enjoys silence. And it rises with an agreeable determination to the challenge of tensions, crises and no-win dilemmas.

AUTHORITY

There is a kind of power given neither by control, by office, nor by prestige, and it can't be achieved by ambition. Reputation is some of it, but only some. This is the power of authority.

The nature of this kind of power, where it comes from, how it can be recognized, the ways it works—these are questions that stock answers cannot satisfy. For instance, authority may come with older age, although that is not assured, since the seniors in our society may not carry the authority of clan elders. The accoutrements of age, such as the dyed hair, dentures and wrinkles of a person in a retirement beach chair, do not confer the same authority as do similar signs (scars, lines, toothlessness and tattoos) in the face of a tribal elder. Age is not enough. Nor does the maxim "information is power" hold for authority. A person may be crammed with data and remember all the intrigue and personal history of the office, proving "invaluable" to the company, and never gain enough authority to be heard.

Authority may come from exceptional accomplishment, but that, too, is not assured, for specific expertise does not necessarily confer the wider weight of respect. Field experience may contribute to authority, but armchair reflection may prove proportionately more significant. Therefore, the frequent use of experts on TV as "authorities" confuses the narrow with the broad, opinion with sagacity, and information with knowledge. The voice of authority on Eastern Europe or education policy called to the TV panel need not be limited to field hands "who have been there" when what is wanted is that old mental virtue called estimation, the capacity to make value judgments by seeing not just all the angles but also seeing deeply into the long-term roots and ramifications of an issue. Speaking to the essential issue differs from speaking for or against a position in regard to an issue. The authoritative voice brings an intrinsic quality of disinterest—with conviction.

This quality is hard to describe, yet like good art and bad pornography (or bad art and good pornography), "I know it when I see it." It may be lodged anywhere in almost anyone, though actual examples are few. We come across it in memory—someone in your hometown childhood, a person of dignity who could size things up and whose words struck deep, whose mere presence appreciated invisible values. Was it what she did; what he said? Was it how they carried themselves, or reacted at a critical moment? Was it their aura of distance or their easiness, so at home in the world? One thing seems sure: they made you feel the power of authenticity. They simply had it in themselves.

Even if authority arises as an autonomous gift and resides in my specific nature, its actual power manifests only within a communal context. It must be recognized. I may be experienced, intelligent, unique and detached, but until I am needed, until my voice is called for, I do not have authority.

Other people grant the authority that cannot be conferred by individuality alone. Authority is therefore societal, just as self is communal. We belong to each other, and the recognition by others of the qualities that each person embodies is as basic to human awareness as is the recognition of cries and songs among birds and smells among mammals. Authority may be intrinsic, but it is not really there until given confirmation by the world. "World," by the way, is not confined only to other people; for authority in humans is recognized also by animals, who show quickly whom they respect and whom among their handlers they can trick, scare and disobey.

That authority cannot be affected by persuasion and does not try to tyrannize or even subordinate shows its intrinsic autonomy. This autonomy is less a sign of aloofness than of radical independence from all other kinds of power. The radical independence of judicial courts written into the Constitution separates judgment from other kinds of power. It must be disinterested. Perhaps it is in this very independence from the usual manifestations of power that the authority of authority lies.

The misuse of the term "authorities" for governing

bodies, of "authoritarianism" for despotism, and diagnosing an "authority problem" as a rebellious inability to take direction defame the idea of authority and confuse it with other styles of power.

This confusion of an authoritative voice with an authoritarian one shows how little we grasp this kind of power. It also shows how fearful we are of authority in a democratic society, and one increasingly egalitarian. But even more, these confusions tell how ego-centered are our notions of power in general; we seem unable to imagine authority as a gift or capacity not located in the ego. So what limits our understanding here is not fear of authority but the justified fear of usurpation of it by the ego.

I want to stress the detachment of this kind of power, its inner restraint, for authority gives enormous power. One voice can sway a thousand. The respect afforded by others raises you above others. A potential for tyranny is always there the moment you exercise your authority. Shakespeare writes (*Measure for Measure* II, ii, 108): "O! it is excellent / To have a giant's strength, but it is tyrannous / To use it like a giant." Withholding, disinterestedness, independence seem to be necessary corollaries of authority.

The independence of authority frees it from the office, prestige and trappings of power. Bernard Baruch had only a park bench; Wendell Berry keeps to his poems and his Kentucky farm. Einstein. Segovia. Casals. Rouault. Matisse. Recent pop psychology that wants to give back to

men the authority they feel they've lost refers to this independence as the inner king. In a play that treats the lost
power of a king, Shakespeare says a lot in a few lines about
authority. When Kent places himself in service to the king,
Lear interviews him for the job *(King Lear* I, iv, 24ff.):

> *"What wouldst thou?"*
>
> *"Service."*
>
> *"Who wouldst thou serve?"*
>
> *"You."*
>
> *"Dost thou know me, fellow?"*
>
> *"No, sir; but you have that in your contenance which I
> would fain call master."*
>
> *"What's that?"*
>
> *"Authority."*

And this is after the king has been deposed from ruling
power. Clearly Lear's authority is intrinsic, and as the play
proceeds and his helplessness and madness increase, the
power of authority never leaves him.

Of course, some of it comes from his past performance. After all he was the king, as Oedipus at the end of
his life, blind, aged, impoverished and dying, still was once
Oedipus Tyrannos. The past is still there in the present.

In our times Averell Harriman, though not to be
measured against figures like Lear and Oedipus, into his
nineties was a man of authority. Without office, without a
power base, his generation of influence long past, he nonetheless still carried authority. Having been an ambassador,

a governor, a special emissary and troubleshooter, a scion of a privileged family, and present at decisive moments of twentieth-century history, of course conferred power on him. But there are many others who "have been there since the beginning" yet fade into oblivion. Authority is more than knowledge, memory, judgment, competence, social relations; more than who you know and where you've been. And because it is an invisible quality, it also attracts great envy and its authenticity is demeaned as merely, in Harriman's case, deriving from wealth or belonging to the right class.

One final component needs to be singled out: what the Romans called *gravitas,* a certain weight that gives importance, even an oppressive seriousness. Descendants of *gravitas* appear in our "gravity" and "grave" and in the French *gravide* for pregnant. *Gravitas* itself descends from an even older, though still most popular, Sanskrit term, *guruh,* weighty. The power of authority comes from the belly; its direction is earthward like gravity.

Perhaps, authority rises as the soul sinks gravely— graveward—as one becomes an ancestor, a figure who represents the stored wisdom of the community, a representation rather than a personality. One's authority comes then less from personal history and more from impersonal authorities beyond the grave, the dead and their teachings. Is that why we turn in crises and in older age to biographies, trying to deepen our individual personality by connecting with the past and the dead, those figures Emerson called Representative Men? And perhaps that's why authority seems most apparent in the aging. Maybe it is ultimately authorized by the chthonic gods of the Underworld, by Hades, and the ancestors whom our culture recognizes only as History.

PERSUASION

Tough guys on TV have changed the meaning of persuasion and its kind of power. Persuasion has come to mean literal arm-twisting—the use of cruel force, Mafia style. Or police brutality to wring a confession. Our civilization has moved far away from persuasion's home in Latin, for both Suada and Peitho (persuasion in Greek) were Goddesses, and *suadeo* means "make sweet or pleasant," the way a suave lover knows the art of sweet talk and how to give pleasure to make life smooth and agreeable.

In the Greek world, Peitho mainly appears as a distinct figure or as an attribute in association with the Goddesses Athene and Aphrodite. Persuasion is mainly a power of seduction, by means of intelligent convincing speech (Athene) or by charm of manner and beauty of figure (Aphrodite). The greatest gift of Peitho is rhetoric, the gift of gab.

Advertisers recognize that different products and different audiences call for different rhetorics. You do not sell secondhand cars and bargain mattresses the same way you advertise perfumes or douches or cruises to the Caribbean. There are styles of persuasion, styles of rhetorical dis-

guises. Advertising in its infancy in the last century per-
suaded mainly by disguising itself as education. The commercial messages were directed at a vast immigrant
population, teaching them the modes of progress. Progress
as canned fruit, condensed milk, packaged soap. "New and
improved" is a leftover phrase of the persuasive rhetoric of
progress.

Advertisements are not the only place where the ancient force of this Goddess still holds sway, seducing us to
go and get, buy and do what often seems far from our
character and unrooted in our desire. Peitho appears also
as a power in one of the serious phobias of daily life. The
statistics of psychological stress report that the fear of
speaking in public is a major inhibition impeding the advancement up the corporate and governmental ladders.
Despite the talk shows, the call-in programs, the public
town meetings and the explosion of electronic messages,
phones and internets, not everyone evidently is in good
graces with Peitho and cannot find the ways and means to
persuasively express themselves. Talk without charm,
without mind, without care for its beauty and desire to
affect another person's passion fills the air and ear with
dead verbiage. Talk as violence. Talk as anesthesia. Talk as
pollution. Its only persuasive power is that it makes one get
out of range or turn it off.

In public life those who talk simple and tough, and
mean rather than sweet, like Ross Perot, are more convincing than those who stand well with Peitho, as Mario

Cuomo does. Men with little verbal grace can in our civilization still rise to high office—for instance, Coolidge, Eisenhower, Nixon, Bush, Mondale, Quayle. Speech that can move others and thus be an agency of power need not be flowery or flattering, but it must attempt at least some turn of phrase, affect some beauty (Aphrodite) and exhibit intelligence and civic idealism (Athene). I am thinking of the persuasive power of Lincoln, Woodrow Wilson and Franklin Roosevelt. They each had that persuasive capacity to alter the destiny of a nation by the way they put words together, their power of rhetoric. To explain and defend a policy, to relate and to communicate requires more than charts, quips and anecdotes. Neither charisma, authority, training in public appearances, nor mastery of a field of facts will reach the audience, unless your language carries conviction so that it can convince others.

Hardly a generation or two ago the presidents of banks and the captains of industry and trade, who had graduated from college, usually held degrees not in business administration, economics or technology, but in English. English majors provided the corporate managerial class. A major in English was the major road to the top. Why?

Unlike knowledge of a specific subject matter such as finance or engineering, the refinement of rhetoric gained in English classes taught the organization of thought concerning *any* subject matter. This meant that a graduate in English could speak sentences that held thought, could express views and decisions convincingly, analyze written materials, distinguish major from minor questions, uncover buried assumptions and illogical consequences, as well as find the felicitous phrases that made the atmosphere at work pleasant and agreeable.

Persuasion was and is a managerial talent that turns away the wrath of stockholders, union leaders, creditors, reporters and government inspectors. It softens firing, facilitates borrowing and wins contracts. And it raises the level of discourse throughout the entire enterprise. Persuasive rhetoric is indeed a necessary kind of power.

The need for this power was long acknowledged. During the Middle Ages and the Renaissance, rhetoric was a principal component of higher education. Power required style in words; language that could convince had to be forged. And our civilization still lives on the formulations of ancient Church Fathers, medieval physicians and judges, the rhetoric of the Magna Carta and the King James Bible, as it still relies on the resounding phrases of the Declaration of Independence and the Constitution composed more than two hundred years ago and which continue to retain their persuasive force.

Terms like "sheer rhetoric" and "empty rhetoric" show the disdain we have for fancy speech and the bias we cherish for plain, puritan, tell-it-like-it-is English. Especially, monosyllables and curt phrases that imply action, though they are more commands than persuasions. "Come and get it," "just do it," "no problem," "wake up," "enjoy," "take it off," "start now," "get going," "buy, sell or hold" are captions rather than seductions. Yet a chief executive must take great care not to lose touch with this kind of abrupt common parlance by displaying a flair for nuanced speech.

It is not truly difficult to distinguish "empty rhetoric" from the persuasive power of speech given by the Goddess. Sheer rhetoric has the flowers but strikes no roots in deeper soil. It is only the prettying of shallow thought, principally by the use of clichés and jargons, whether Hallmark sympathy, New Age global wistfulness or business boosterism. It neither surprises, challenges nor seduces. Listening to empty rhetoric, we have the feeling we've heard it all before, and many times. The real thing lifts you to your feet and turns your head, the course of your life permanently swayed toward a new direction—just by the power of words.

CHARISMA

A charismatic person is one blessed with grace given by the Gods—that's what "charisma" originally meant. As a gift of the Gods, however, it does not belong to the innate structure of personality, that animal-like quality I have been describing as leadership. Charisma may fall on anyone, even on those in whom the ability to lead and to bear authority are woefully absent, thereby deceiving followers who cannot distinguish mastery from magic.

Neither money nor the media can confer charisma. It is a grace apart from popular fame, celebrity, outstanding accomplishment, royal blood and oodles of gold. You may be a Letterman, a Leno or a Larry and yet not be alive with charisma even though your ratings go up and your fans keep the faith. Charismatic power lends splendor to the showman, at moments raising his status to the shaman. He feels "on," hot, cool, in the zone, with it—but none of this power belongs to him nor can it be recharged by superstitious rites or by intoxicants. We might like to attribute charisma to a type of personality—the genius or the psychopathic. Yet as these two terms themselves suggest, this kind of power is a mystery that does not belong to human persons but enhances them with an otherworldly charm that is best expressed by the term "star."

If leadership arises from an instinctual base and authority from character, charisma partly depends on situations. A situation requires someone to symbolize and articulate its dynamics. Think of Boris Yeltsin standing up to the tanks, of General MacArthur snatching a psychological victory from the jaws of defeat with one phrase: "I shall return." Charisma may also suddenly illumine a corporation, as it fell upon Apple Computer, and upon IBM long ago.

The charismatic person exemplifies what is taking place. History is full of, is even made by, these archetypal incarnations who represent the spirit of the age, of the times or of only a singular moment. Johnny-on-the-spot: here and now becomes a human being. He or she may appear from a distance like Napoleon from Corsica and Franco from North Africa, out of political exile like de Gaulle and Churchill, or simply out of nowhere, and become the walking-around embodiment of a great historical scene. As strangely as they come onto the stage, so they often vanish once their scene is played out, remaining marvelous in memory or discredited as charlatans. It is as if an archetypal mantle wraps a human person in a golden aura of transcendent power—and it may have nothing at all to do with previous biography.

Charismatic figures usually do not rise through the ranks, like a new chief who was formerly a loyal vice president in charge of marketing. Usually, their elevation is a surprise. But when they appear, problems disappear. A stroke of luck, an unforeseen deal, disaster averted. A charismatic personality may also help the corporate image in public relations. They show well in the media. But charisma doesn't handle labor negotiations, restructuring for a turnaround or petty struggles with a querulous board. As Gods give gifts, they also take them away, and they do not seem to care much about the balance sheet. So problems return when the Gods have gone, leaving only an all too human CEO.

Charisma can be a crucial factor. Thomas Dewey, brilliant prosecuting attorney and effective governor of New York, had power aplenty—prestige, influence, control, office—but he had no charisma. He lost elections to both Roosevelt and Truman. John Lindsay had plenty, and maybe that was all he had, for as mayor of New York City in the sixties he is still blamed for its fiscal insolvency thirty years later. Ronald Reagan's Teflon charisma could hold an entire nation, even its Congress and its media, starry-eyed during the severe unemployment of his first term and the cynical corruption during his second.

If the charismatic figure has no authority, then we see an emperor without clothes, in no way up to the symbolic load to be carried. If the figure is without innate leadership, then the crowd ennobles a fool and follows charisma to its own ruin. With *both* authority *and* leadership, however, charisma changes history—through such persons as Joan of Arc, Napoleon, Martin Luther King, Jr., Robert E. Lee, Abraham Lincoln and Charles de Gaulle.

Rising

What seems merely to be personal ambition, rather ruthless and a cover-up for feelings of inferiority, may lie deeper. What is "The force that through the green fuse drives the flower . . . The force that drives the water through the rocks . . ."? Dylan Thomas, who wrote the famous poem, says in the same lines that we are "dumb" to this force. We cannot account for the green push upward of nature. We are like dumb animals. What can we say in respect to the force that drives the horse to lead, the one kitten to nuzzle ahead of the litter?

In the oldest Chinese text, an oracle book called the *I Ching* (Wilhelm-Baynes translation) or *Yi Ching* (Ritsema-Karcher new translation), the first of the sixty-four chapters discusses the rising power of yang and the animal elaborated is the dragon. The text reads:

The movement of heaven is full of power.

Thus the superior man makes himself strong and untiring.

The force of which we can give no account is the "movement of heaven" beyond human motives and personality structure. It is a movement in the cosmos itself that comes at certain times and to certain people in certain situations, and its effects can be heroic, every obstacle yielding before the force that carries you like a flying dragon, like riding a swollen river. Its effects can also be arrogance, inflation, conceit and fanaticism. These moments of the rising spirit offer the extraordinary ability to do. "I'm on a roll," we say. "Full of power," says the ancient text in the very first image with which the whole Chinese book begins.

Fateful situations can release the river, the sudden power surge—the death of a parent and inheritance of one's territory, a big revelatory dream, apostolic succession when you are advanced to a higher station, or winning in love, at the track, a game, an election. It can come as a flood of eros and as unannounced as a red rock-hard erection.

But this rising with wings, this riding the swollen river, should not be reduced to phallic tumescence or to the willful exertion of force. The lead horse does not run because it is whipped. For the river—"sullen, untamed, intractable" (T. S. Eliot)—ruts its course through the terrain in its own blindly headstrong way, and you are not a river. You have eyes, it hasn't; it merely goes.

All living things have a fermenting hidden heat, once imagined as a solarlike energy and later equated with the combustion of oxygen. This hidden heat breaks out in fevers and rashes, in furies and rages. It rises to our heads and drives us out of our minds, as if we were possessed by sheer power. Michael Meade, in a remarkable chapter on the necessity of initiation in youth, describes this rising power in terms of what the Gisu people of Uganda call the *Litima*.

Meade writes: "To them [the Gisu], Litima is the violent emotion peculiar to the masculine part of things that is the source of quarrels, ruthless competition, possessiveness, power-driveness, and brutality and that is also the source of independence, courage, upstandingness, and meaningful ideals. Litima names and describes the willful emotional force that fuels the process of becoming an individual . . . Litima is ambiguous . . . it has two sides. The source of independence and high ideals can also be the source of ruthlessness and brutality"*

Rising is not a focused power, it is more a heightened level of energy and heightened irritability, a feeling of compression, ready to explode with a head full of plans, too much to do, the body racing. This emotion psychiatry calls the submanic mood, one important diagnostic sign of which is being "strong and untiring," as the Chinese text says. There is a dragon in the blood.

Now, a dragon is a mythical animal, an animal wholly imaginal. It breathes fire, gleams green, has many heads, protects treasures, and it also eats humans, especially beautiful ones, young ones, and those that are naively heroic. Because it is an animal wholly imaginal, we are enthralled through our own animal power of imagination. Imagination

---

* Michael Meade, *Men and the Water of Life,* San Francisco: Harper San Francisco, 1993, pp. 233–34.

working us like an animal force, giving us head trip after head trip, burning our close surroundings and making us feel that we are coiled protectively around unnamable gifts. Our humanity is eaten by a force that drives the water through the rock. And so we are too dumb to give account of what is happening, dumb in the double sense of speechless and stupid. We are in the sway of myth, myth as instinctual drive that carries us on its back like a dragon. Maybe this is why, since our culture lacks effective initiations, we need so desperately to have colleagues, friends, habits, wives and husbands, sandwiches and laundry, parking lots and hardware stores to save us from the rising, or if not save us, at least provide a place to land.

DECISION

"Can't make up his mind." "Won't come down on either side." "Paralyzed by indecision." These condemnations express all too clearly the importance of decisiveness for the exercise of power. Decision releases power; perhaps, as the very essence of agency, decision is power. A decision by the Supreme Court of the United States supersedes an executive order by the President and a law passed by the Congress.

It is comfortably believed that decisions result from a full briefing. Once all the angles are considered, all eventualities foreseen, decision follows. It is as if decision were a matter of weighing pros and cons in the balancing scales of judgment. This view of decision making gives too much credit to reason. Decisions come as much from the gut, from a chance bit of data or gossip, from intuitive hunches, from the still small voice of what I am elsewhere calling "the angel," as they come from long pondering a well-written digest of the facts.

Decision's root *(caedo, caedere)* means striking down. The first Latin meaning is hardly rational. It exclaims brute power: "to strike, smite, beat." The second meaning ties *caedo, caedere* with sexual intercourse, as we witness any day when birds mate. A third meaning is: "to kill, slay, murder; to attack, slaughter in sacrifice"; a fourth: "to crack, smash, break." *Caedo* itself goes back to Sanskrit *khidati,* "press," *kheda,* "hammer."

When the gavel strikes to end the market's trading day, conclude an auction or bring to a close the court's proceedings, there is an echo of sudden, even violent, death. No going back. So little wonder our agonizing indecisions, for decision brings death into the scene, and the person who can make a decision—like Kennedy alone before the Bay of Pigs, like Eisenhower alone before D-Day deciding to give the go-ahead order despite the uncertain weather—is in the presence of death, with whom there are no deals, no compromises. No wonder in the more ordinary business of life it is so difficult to bring about a decisive closing, whether by a jury, a legislature, a real estate agent or a salesman.

Decisiveness is necessary to create. The dictionary says the tenth meaning of *caedo* is to create by cutting. Each of the tiniest actions in the arts requires decisions—to include and to exclude, to move this way or that, to select this first and that later. Every movie we see and book we read is a creation made by cutting. Decision knows when and where to stop, to let the moment of death conclude a work. A painting teacher once told a friend of mine that the thing she finds most important in teaching the art of painting is when to stop the painting, when to cut, close, end.

The creativity of decision shows first of all as the capacity to move forward out of irresolution and ambivalence. However, at the same moment that we let loose action by our decision we also create enemies. Decisions divide. They cut in two. To decide, says the Oxford English Dictionary, means "to determine by giving the victory to one side or the other." Each decision leaves a loser and builds shadow feelings in an organization. The defeated party becomes the injured party and seeks redress of what it feels are the wrongs arising from a "wrong" decision. Disaffection. Subversive resistance. Revenge builds in the corridors of power. Since each victory means more unwilling captives of that decision, power built on decisiveness can lead to tyranny. Alexander of Macedon and the generals of the Roman Empire knew that victory creates only more enemies and so they took as slaves or exterminated the remnants of the defeated, tore apart their cities and temples stone for stone, salted their earth. The demand for unconditional surrender aims to eliminate forever the shadow possibility of revenge that lies latent after a decisive victory.

Leaders today take comfort in the belief that we've put Greece and Rome behind us. We today prefer consensus decisions rather than victories. We believe in compromises, that the other side can be brought around or bought off. The deal has replaced victory and defeat, and so decisions are today hammered out more subtly, letting everyone have a piece of the action by buying the right legal language. Therefore, decisions are more likely to be headed off before a decisive crisis comes to a head—that is, the person in charge tries to avoid bringing down the hammer on one side or the other, in favor of forging differing constituencies into larger unities with vague edges and mush words. This tactic is as ancient as the empire of China and as contemporary as the White House of Clinton. The heroic sword that cuts issues into two warring camps calls the tactic waffling, wavering and fence straddling. Nonetheless these hesitations show a wary awareness of the pitfalls of all decisiveness. It can be its own undoing because of the accumulated defeats created by decisiveness itself.

The seemingly indecisive tactics of trimming the sails with the wind follows from a prior decision: to avoid decision at all costs, and this trimming and shifting must be distinguished from neurotic indecisiveness. By this I mean holding oneself and others in suspension in order to hold on to power. I can stay in control by indecision just as cleverly as by risking a decision. There is a narcissistic use of indecision that makes one the center of attention as everyone in the king's court waits and wonders what will be decided. The longer one can hesitate, call in counsels for consultations, hold policy roundtables and read determination papers from committees of experts, the more important seems to be both the decision and one's own position within the decision-making process.

In short, there are at least three varieties of indecision that may look much alike: first, timidity, being reluctant to slice through with the sword because one fears the exposure and the risks consequent upon cutting; second, prudent wisdom that foresees the aftermath of a decision; third, neurotic wavering in order to keep one's prestige and stay in office. When hesitating about a decision, it can be useful to examine ruthlessly the intermixing of these three motives. But even self-examination calls for a decision.

FEARSOMENESS

It was said of General, later President, Andrew Jackson that he "got the most out of his men because they feared him more than they feared the enemy." The exercise of power through fear still accomplishes what other styles cannot. TV teaches this lesson every day. Neither the badge of office nor the voice of authority gets action as quickly as the threat of truncheon and gun. Effective agency seems to require fear. Have you not heard that "a manager may be loved but must be feared?" Control-and-command management knows well the uses of fear.

A university administrator explained carefully to me that by predicting financial disasters and scandalous embarrassments he could move his lethargic supervisory boards and academic committees to make decisions. "I had to make them afraid; it's definitely the best method for overcoming institutional inertia."

The ability to instill fear belongs to the full panoply of power. Of all the faces of power, fearsomeness seems to serve as a profound stabilizing principle. To the kinds of dynamics that hold vast empires together, like language, culture, economics and geography, must be added fear as a building force of commonality. Shared fear unifies peoples. Even in our century the two superpowers with their accumulated potential of unimaginable devastation were held at bay for decades by the fear of mutually assured destruction (MAD). The recent long period of major world peace was granted by fear.

The idea of fearsomeness reveals a cause of tyranny's hold. Fearsomeness belongs mythically to the world of Ares/Mars, lord of battle rage, one of whose two sons was named Phobos (fear), from which our "phobic" and "phobia." Other Gods of war in other cultures and sculptured guardians at temple gates in Asia show fearsome faces, warding off the false reverence of piousness, sentimentality and empty ceremony. The emotion of fear corresponds with the facts of power; close to power, only a fool is not afraid. Many symptoms appearing in offices and factories called stress, incontinence, slowdown and absenteeism are the paralyzing or panicked reactions of fear to the fearsomeness of power in the workplace. Panic attacks and anxiety states unconsciously recognize the fearsomeness of power.

Not cleanliness, but fearsomeness, is truly next to godliness, since the Bible teaches that the fear of the Lord is the beginning of wisdom. Yet no one speaks well of fear even if some of us, and some hidden parts of us, can delight in its pleasure. There is a pleasure in being fearsome. Imagine the drill sergeant, the prison guard, the champion boxer, the tough and haughty teenage ice maiden or the terrifying middle-aged son at last able to keep his old parent cowed. Imagine the family life of millions whose power relations are structured by the most fearsome member. Someone in these families has found that the route to pleasure goes via fear. Abused victims who have discovered the pleasures of masochism understand the uses of fear for excitation, increased sensitivity and imaginative awareness.

Unless we are willing to entertain the idea that causing fear gives pleasure, we can never grasp the full depths of power. The documented cases of torture the world over by Amnesty International attest not only to the universality of human depravity but to the universal pleasure of arousing fear. Men and women frighten and torture other men and women, animals and things as part of their everyday jobs; the career of fear must give satisfaction beyond the call of duty. Horror and crime movies, of course, capitalize on the fear associated with power. Every raised voice and menacing look, every glinting gun and fistfight raises the heartbeat of the audience, so that we cannot tell, sitting there in the dark, what is masterful authority, despotic tyranny or just plain fear. In *The Unforgiven,* named as one of the twenty best films ever, the distinction among kinds of power becomes clearer. Clint Eastwood and Gene Hackman are both ruthless killers, and though Hackman wears the badge of office, he commands by means of fearsomeness; Eastwood, a broken-down pig farmer, displays the power of authority.

The fascination with cruelty and the instigation of fear seem lodged in the essence of human character, not only in Americans and not only in those deprived or abused. Children thrill with pleasure in hearing tales of torture, telling frightening ghoulish stories and watching horrible images on television. The term medical psychology gave to the erotics of fear (sadism) which binds victim and violator—and viewer—derives from the Marquis de Sade, whose work explores this sort of power in its furthest imaginative range.* What Sade attempted is the dissociation of sensibility, detaching erotic pleasure from the usual feelings of beauty, love and genital fascination in order to expose the erotic connection of pleasure with the power of fear.

The Buddha supposedly said that all things are in fear, even plants and stones. This fundamental fact gives his *mudra* (gesture) of "fear not" such cosmic significance. Fearsomeness comes with the universe, belonging to cosmic predation. Everything eats away at everything else in an intricate interlocking system from which there is no escape; a system that we have conveniently, idealistically, sterilized with the name "biosphere," which also states that everything is usable. That all things are in service to one another in cosmic mutuality—or cosmic predation— means that everything is exploitable. This is a fearsome idea, but isn't it implied in the very nature of power?

* Cf. Thomas Moore, *Dark Eros: The Imagination of Sadism* (Dallas: Spring Publications, 1990).

TYRANNY

I shall make tyrannical use of this one term. Under it
I want to include subjugation, despotism, aggrandizement,
dominion, exploitation. John Locke, the seventeenth-cen-
tury English philosopher, defined tyranny most clearly as
"an Absolute, Arbitrary Power one Man has over another
to take away his Life whenever he pleases." We are re-
turning again to our opening premise, subordination, now
in an extreme form. Descriptions of tyranny usually include the willful exercise of absolute sovereignty, arbitrary
justice or none at all, and cruel, harsh and persecutory
rule. The prohibition of "cruel and unusual punishments"
by the Eighth Amendment to the Constitution was one the
American precautions against the return of tyranny.

The key word in the definitions of tyranny from its
first use by the Greeks until today is "absolute," indicating
that tyranny does not so much require a single monarch or
dictator as *singleness of mind* literalized as a single absolute
ruler. Tyranny can rule by a group like a Politburo, a
Directory, a religious order, a royal or Mafia family so long
as the members do not differ in principle or in the implementation of principle. The supremacy of a dogma and the

single aim of party line, of aggrandizement of the family or the junta of colonels, count more than the exemplar of tyranny in a single person. Absolutism is not a ruthless ruler, but a ruthless rule—and this we don't easily remember, for our minds fix upon the figures of czars and crime lords. These images serve to keep the danger of tyranny projected onto Stalin, Genghis Khan and Al Capone, protecting us from the absolutism that can rule the psyche in the guise of fundamentalism in religion, bottom-lineism in business and progress in the sciences.

Besides, the projection of tyranny onto fearsome tyrants defends us against an even closer insight: absolutism can rule our personal lives. We live under tyranny unawares. One point of view, one faith, one set way of doing things can aggrandize and exploit all others in our natures until we are subject to absolute rules that soon act autonomously. Freud's psychology called these dominants "dictates of the superego." Many symptoms express the tyranny of these fixed rules. Cramps and spasms, clenchings and arthritic aches, circulatory and excretory inhibitions refer often to the obstinacy of chronic habits which cannot let go their rules and just give over. It is as if the old mythical figure of severe and rigid melancholy, Saturn, had become the psyche's absolute ruler. Dutiful endurance; aged before one's time. Meanwhile, other acute symptoms like eruptions, accidents and breakdowns may be demonstrations of the rebellious oppressed suddenly rising to confront the absolutism of habitual consciousness.

Habitual consciousness must suppress in order to focus. To exist among the buzzing informational input that assails us, we select and repress. We adhere to what works for us. What works becomes a privileged way of doing things, soon the *only* way of doing things. As we get older, and more blind, this tyranny of habitual consciousness becomes more and more visible to others. Daniel Goleman's study of how we are deceived by our own habitual consciousness shows that tyrannical one-sided rule is the basis of self-deception.*

This kind of power, which makes us both effective and blind, goes deeper than merely being set in our ways. It is the tyrannical rule of style, the style of our thinking and working and connecting, the style of our words and gestures, and as it all fits together into the integrated personality, consciousness becomes tyrannical. We drink to escape from this tyrant; divorce, fall in love, quit jobs, move residences, go bankrupt, shoot rapids, hang-glide, fight our children—anything to escape the cruel and unusual punishment inflicted by the absolutism of successful rule. Everything has been subordinated to the one tyrannical pattern. All otherness gone. One has become totally oneself and now one suffers from totalitarian rule.

Inasmuch as every organization, including that group of odd fellows and leading ladies who compose each human psyche, is a multiple association, the rule of one will al-

* Daniel Goleman, *Vital Lies, Simple Truths: The Psychology of Self-Deception* (New York: Simon & Schuster, 1985).

ways be menaced by other feelings and other viewpoints. The more we insist on words like "integration," "unity" and "centeredness," and the more we imagine that power comes from "getting it all together," the more likely growth becomes aggrandizement of the one over the others and development becomes simply exploitation.

Tyranny ultimately rests on a carrying myth, an inner conviction given by an archetypal force. For instance, the myth of the hero who can overcome all obstacles; the myth of the divinely inspired and protected child who can run unlimited risks and who skateboards through life without any afterthoughts; the myth of romantic sexual passion that inspires beyond the human even to its destruction. But myths don't get much credit in our profit-and-loss accounting of life. We believe only in those myths that are presented as facts and truths, like neo-Darwinian competition. Since myths go unrecognized we live them, or they live us, blindly. In this blindness we are each, as Freud said, enacting Oedipus, the tyrant, who could not see what myth he was living on, and dying from.

The ancient cure for tyranny was tyrannicide—kill the king; another is popular democracy—giving each adult voice a vote. A third cure is the complex table of organization with separation of executive powers, vetoes and comptrollers, ethics committees, investigating ombudsmen and special prosecutors, overlapping bureaucracies and interlocking directorates—all codified into the intricacies of a legal system.

Still another cure is ritual reference to a pantheon of powers. This was the polytheistic method that ruled the ancient world and many cultures outside the monotheisms that worship a single all-supreme being—tyranny made in heaven. History and anthropology both show clearly that the polytheistic cure doesn't guarantee freedom from political tyranny, yet for psychological reasons it's worth considering.

The pantheon was so structured that Zeus/Jupiter, for instance, was merely first among equals *(primus inter pares)*. He could not trespass into the domains of other Olympians. This constraint goes further than the notion of limited monarchy, because absolutism cannot be restrained merely by sharing power with an oligarchy. Nor can it be limited by law. Tyranny begins by suborning law or bending it to its use. Because the idea of a pantheon corresponds with the inner structure of the psyche, it can offer restraint where tyranny originates—that is, in the mind's fantasy of itself as an absolute and solitary governor. The dictionary, by the way, defines "absolute" as without condition, limitation or obligation; independent, disengaged. It is absolved of relations—unfettered, a freewheeling agent. The tyrannical mind believes in its own power; it "makes up its own mind."

But the idea of a pantheon refuses to let the mind believe in itself so absolutely. It says that the mind, like everything in the world, is composite and subject to many powers, each with different myths calling for continual observation. A human being is imagined less as a central agent in whom, by definition, tyranny is always a possibility, and more as a field in flux in which friction between figures requires rituals of reflective questioning.

That's why other cultures are always consulting the stars, rain clouds, birds, the innards of animals, portents and omens, much as we watch economic forecasts before making a major move. What once were, and elsewhere are, diviners and soothsayers, here are statisticians, actuaries, chartists and economic prognosticators. The magic of trends. The difference between the two rituals lies in the focus of the procedures. Ours seeks by gathering data to empower the mind's rule over the confusion of circumstance and put them in order. Theirs seeks to differentiate and empower the others, so that things will fall into a cosmic order. That's also why belief is central to our approach and sacrifice central to theirs. Instead of being cast in the image of a single omnipotent God as in our culture, the human being in these other cultures reflects contesting voices and is imagined to be always in a nexus of relations. So I am always obliged to ask "Who is in command now?" Which principle, which myth, which power has now usurped the throne and is making up my mind?

Rituals of reflective questioning empower the others, as with a dream interpretation. I not only watch what the "I" does or does not do, but what are the others doing, and who are *they,* and why are they there in "my" dream at all? The first question in a polytheistic model of the psyche is about the others, as it was in Greece when consulting an oracle. They asked not, "What's wrong with me?" or "What should I do now?" They asked, "To which God or Goddess do I turn in this situation?" Who now has the power? That simple question—"Who?"—announces that I am not in sole command and that my tyrannical potential has been put in question.

VETO

This singular kind of power demonstrates agency dedicated wholly to negation. Its sole strength lies in its ability to frustrate the will of the many. Although granted by the many to the one, by the collective to the individual as a protective guarantee, the veto asserts an equality between the one and the group. The fact that the majority will of Congress can be annulled by the veto of a single President increases the power of the one equal to that of the many. The veto thus forms part of what the American system of constitutional government calls "the balance of powers."

The veto offers no positive alternatives, no compromise, and it is not subject to conditions. It can only be overridden by the power of an even greater majority. Its power is wholly prohibitive, as the word from the Latin means: "I forbid."

That the veto is built into systems of government at the highest level—United Nations Security Council, the American presidency—shows a profound recognition of the importance of negativity and suggests that negation is fundamental to the power of power.

Negation, said Freud, is repression: "A negative judgment is the intellectual substitution for repression; the 'no' in which it is expressed is the hallmark of repression." What huge power resides in that little word "no"! It severs relations, refuses cooperation and declares rejection. Anyone who has suffered even the gentlest "no" comes away from the encounter crushed, whether at a business meeting, a dance or in bed. A child of two on first discovering his or her veto power can use it to thwart the will of an entire family and throw its organization into wild disorder. The single syllable offers ultimate control, repressing the intentions of the community, bringing the wheel to a stop.

This amazing strength in the tiny body of the two-year-old attests to sources beyond the human will, and therefore the capacity to say "no" belongs among our congenital traits, a gift or instinct given with nature and innate to all. "Ere the child has seen the light, the principle of beard and gray hairs is innate. Albeit small and hidden, all the functions of the whole body and of every succeeding period of life are there." Here, the Roman writer and philosopher Seneca is referring to the archetypal influences of the Gods, in this case old Saturn, the great frustrater, negator and lord of repression. If the veto does refer to more than human will, the forbidding "no" speaks with the voice of an immense and eternal mythical figure. Indeed, it can give to the single individual a weight that balances out the will of the majority. Perhaps because of its Saturnian negativity, many Presidents hesitate to use the veto as an active measure, preferring to bypass the decisive negative force by means of the "pocket veto."

Veto power cripples. The old Polish Parliament, for example, gave the power of individual veto to every member of the nobility, who, each for his own arbitrary reason or unreason, was able to block measures of the elected government for years and years.

If the most condensed notion of power is "agency that subordinates," then the veto most boldly and clearly exemplifies this power. Subordination, or holding down and back, is precisely what the veto is able to do so well. That same "no" which forbids, however, may also have in sight a long-range positive outcome. For what begins as the last bitter holdout of a declining leader, administration or social class may also be the only course open to a visionary leader who sees but is too far ahead of the pack. Instead of bringing up the rear guard, visionaries ride point into unknown territory. The last remaining option—influence, persuasion, authority all gone—may be to veto the ill-conceived plans of others. The negative judgment expressed by the veto follows Immanuel Kant's insight: "The peculiar province of negative judgments is solely to prevent error." In other words, negation may be motivated by an ideal vision, a purity of purpose in dedication to ideals, so the veto then belongs with the kind of power we next turn to—purism.

PURISM

Tyranny is not the uttermost extreme of subordination. There is still a further, higher step into spiritual purity. This is an idea of power shown rarely though worshipped broadly and formulated in this century by the purity of principle and martyred deaths of two men of huge power, Martin Luther King, Jr., and Mohandas K. Gandhi. That our discussion now has come to this exceptional kind of power shows that we are following the determining ideals of the Western tradition into the realm of spirit. Up is our favorite direction. Remember Jung's definition of the power complex with which this Part began? The key word was "above."

Spirit speaks in absolutes. It subordinates all that is below. It relegates to a lower place whatever does not accommodate to its superior vision. Spirit gives clear commands and always sets sights on higher peaks, no matter how lowly the sphere of its activity, as in the assemblies and marches of both King and Gandhi. There is no place or person too small, for in just that humble modesty does spirit show its overcoming power. It overcomes because it dreams and it foresees; and the followers of spirit, as they climb the ladders toward empowerment, must shed the entanglements and encumbrances of compromised life. All marches are upward toward the better, the future and the true. The true is one and certain, and not double, for double brings doubt.

Classical images of spirit are sunray, arrow and wing, eagle and antler, invisible voice, mountain peak, wind and fire. "Clarity," "order," "truth," "oneness" are some of its favorite terms. The dimension is vertical, the way straight and narrow and the emotion solitary. One single man or woman embodies the way and the goal, like Mao on his march or Joan of Arc in her battles.

This kind of power does not aim to rule over others. Its intention is neither despotism nor even control, but rather it seeks to stand above every other kind of power that is engaged with life. Purity is a tyranny over life itself, showing the power of a single self over the claims of life. Therefore, spiritual power can sleep in the village and walk with the workers because this kind of power is uncontaminated by life's concerns. It stands above money, above prestige and fame. Its authority is supreme, or, better said, supremacy is its authority. The power of purism accumulates through shedding and gathers strength not by expansion but by abnegation. Although it may speak the words of inclusive unity, embracing everyone in its vision, the vision itself is sharp and hard as the edge of a sword, utterly exclusive and uncompromising. Of such people you often hear said: "He never lets up . . . completely dedicated

. . . disciplined . . . so hard on himself . . . he never wavers but knows exactly where he is going." "She is consumed by a mission . . . no one can keep up with her . . . always on top of her work . . . she sure doesn't suffer fools gladly." On the power trip of the pure there is no time for side trips—or tourists.

Singleness of vision—by which purism can be defined —isolates those who carry it. The self that can exhibit power over the demands of life is a loner, sometimes a hermit, sometimes a righteous crusader, hardly different from a fanatic terrorist. Since only death is truly unconcerned with life, thereby wielding ultimate power over it, this kind of power tends its fire in death's cave, drawing power from death and acting as its emissary in the world in the name of the highest values. Purists are deadly, and so they know all about deadly sins.

Although we may admire the purity of spiritual power, and idealize it, we also fear it. This kind of power keeps us at a distance and we shy away from it. Whether it is we who tend to ostracize purists from the intimacy of usual life or it is they who cause their own exile, something happens to keep purism from contamination with the ordinary business of the city street. (And attracts them to "fall" into the arms of prostitution, commercialism and scandal.)

Of all the barriers that surround purism, the psychological ones are the most effective. First, purists of power are called elitists; then, arrogant and aloof; finally, withdrawn and schizoid. The passion they bring with their remedies for life, life itself seems to reject. Too extreme, too radical. Their intolerance of our imperfections is met by our intolerance of their perfection. They are not team players, organization men, brothers and sisters.

Some call the people who incarnate spiritual power "dangerous sociopaths" or "delusional paranoids." Too easily we reach for psychiatric modes of political control, similar to the methods used in the Soviet Union, where dissenters were put in mental hospitals and "treated," as in ours, where the failed are jailed. The categories of abnormal psychology lend themselves readily and virtuously to the state as instruments of its own purism which seeks to keep the body politic immune from alien spiritual infections.

Because the pure in spirit do not submit to the common sense of prevailing consciousness, they seem to have cracked ideas and overly intense ways of behaving. Is this because they believe they *really* could change the world? Television and the popular press (and what press is not popular?) associate them with serial killers and loners who commit hideous crimes against women and children and with "weirdos" who have been abducted by planetary aliens. The status quo musters all its conventional power to harness, castrate, incarcerate and defame purism, at any cost—rightly or wrongly.

Purists of the spirit, whose home is partly out of this world, become enemies of the state because their state of

mind sets them apart as a state unto themselves, as Solzhenitsyn declared himself a state independent of the Soviet
government. Solzhenitsyn, Nobel laureate, had indeed
tended his fires in the cave of death in gulags and cancer
wards. Is not purism, then, the most supreme form of
power? And is this kind of power, for all its tyranny and
self-centered absolutism, not also in service, too, in service to a kind of power we know little about, the power of
the spirits?

SUBTLE POWER

Twenty years of feminist focus on power has shifted many of the usual valences. Today subordination seems an outdated notion belonging to the domination of the males in a patriarchal civilization, as feminists argue. If we follow the feminist argument, then many of the ideas of power we have been describing, such as fearsomeness, tyranny, prestige, control and of course exhibitionism, reflect a "dead white male" civilization and its mummified ideas of power. Moreover, these ideas blind the eye to more subtle kinds of power that function each day to support our getting and doing, our effective agency.

Agency itself, which is the most abstract and impartial of all definitions of power, has become restricted in our civilization to a narrow, vigorous sort of agency modeled on myths of the hero. That solitary muscular individual struggles against evils and devastates enemies; he kills animals and rips through the land, chopping trees and changing the course of rivers. He can carry the whole earth on his shoulders. As our nation anxiously obsesses over competitive productivity, as we aim to become more lean and more mean, our ideas of power have been shaped to conform with this dominating anxiety. Power must be productive and productivity must be heroic.

These vigorous, competitive, athletic notions of power find their support not only in Western myths of the hero but also in Western Christianity. Before monks, before hermits and contemplative saints, before compassionate friars, the early Christians were called "athletes" for Christ. Competition with other sects was how Christianity grew to dominate the eastern Mediterranean or, as we would say today, how it captured the "religious market." The Greek word *athletes* originally meant one who contends, struggles in competitive games and also suffers the trials and tribulations of these struggles. As "athletes," early Christians were zealous missionaries, spreading the word, converting, struggling to achieve deeper "market penetration." The challenges of competition increased Christianity's strength, just as competition is heralded today as the way of keeping a nation productive.

Cannot productive power be imagined differently? Think of the harvest Goddess Demeter/Ceres with her cornucopia stuffed with edible pleasures. Think of the power of feasting in many non-Western societies, where the mark of prestige, authority and leadership, as well as the aim of ambition, is to give away to everyone all they can ever possibly eat.* "Lean and mean" as the main means of productive power neglects the ultimate aim of the

---

* Lewis Hyde, *The Gift: Imagination and the Erotic Life of Property* (New York: Random House/Vintage, 1979).

accumulation of profit in the history of American capitalism. The notable names give it all back: altruism, charity,
endowment, magnanimity. The foundation fathers have become as important in American history as the Founding
Fathers. Must generosity be put off until the end as part of
the last will rather than incorporated into the good will of
daily living?

Philanthropy, which means love of mankind, goes beyond the gifts of money and is not the privilege of only
eminent persons of admirable character. Even the mean
and the miscreant can be philanthropists, exercising power
in daily life by pouring out their vitality in service to their
work or their friends, like Picasso and Ezra Pound. The
power of generosity has little to do with the personal intention of the giver and much to do with the impersonal
effect of the gift. Philanthropy is also a propitiatory rite, an
attempt to give back some of the power that was given to
you lest you become a victim of your own gifts. King
Midas in the old Greek story received the marvelous boon
from Dionysos that whatever Midas touched would become
gold. But as even his food and drink turned to gold, he had
to pray again to Dionysos to take away the very gift that
had made him so rich.

Then there is the power of pleasure. What a dominating hold it has on how we shape our days. I am referring
not only to what we eat and what we wear or how we
spend our evenings. I mean more the power of colors and
tastes, and small talk over our smallest reactions and obser-

vations; the power of sensuousness, wit, affection and friendship—the pleasures that move the body and soul and may well be the final goal of all else we do. Pleasure, like beauty and order, is one of the few great powers that move the cosmos. By recognizing the *Lustprinzip* or pleasure principle that seeks to bring erotic joy to every act to be a force at the root of the soul, Freud ennobled pleasure as a prince of power, not as the Prince of Darkness. That the pleasure principle has been opposed to the work ethic degrades work into slavery and pleasure into childish truancies, causing us to regard pleasure as a decadent parasite sapping the strength of power.

Nowhere does the opposition between work and pleasure become more apparent, and at times absurd, than in the defense of the workplace against the incursions of Aphrodite/Venus in the degraded guise of "sexual harassment." If we imagine that this Goddess of pleasure wants sensuality and erotic fun to find a place everywhere in life, then of course she will seek entrance by hook or by crook into every place where she has been banned. So the question shifts from how to keep sexual harassment from disturbing the workplace to one that asks: Why must the idea of work be so split from pleasure? Why must eros, beauty, dalliance, frivolity, sweetness, sensuality, seduction, charm, flirtation be marginalized to the singles bar and the combat zone so that work may be managed by a puritanical order of "suits" in oxford shirts and cordovan shoes. Myths tell us that any activity, such as office work, which forbids the presence of Aphrodite invites her revenge, and she lives not only in the temples of the past but also in the temple of the soul, that philosophical metaphor for the body.

Enjoy, says the waitress; why not also the boss when you sit down to work? Not only to take pleasure in the work but to give pleasure, like a lover. Isn't this a capacity of power, as much as control, leadership or influence?

What about another sort of agency? Like teaching, like gardening. Or like postoperative nursing. Teachers and gardeners wield immense power in their domains. They dominate and control, yes, with red pencil and pruning clippers; but they do not have to subordinate their charges. A nurse attends an immobile patient; despotism, tyranny, fearsomeness are all potentially present, but her power lies, like the teacher's and the gardener's, in sustaining the life of her charge. The motive and atmosphere of her agency differ radically from the kinds of power we have been reviewing.

Maintenance as the upgrading of energy offers yet another example of sustenance as power. Moreover, you will have surely noticed how many of the activities listed under maintenance—teaching, caring, nursing, cleaning, repairing—have been for so long associated with women or assigned to them as "women's work."

The whole notion of agency needs revision. We have seen only one half. It is as if we have been looking only at the husband in the 1950s marriage who marches off to work while his "little woman" is actually empowering him from behind the front door.

The power to conceive, to carry to term and give birth to, and then nourish, protect and enhance another life shows an everyday kind of incomparable agency, literally as mother and metaphorically as a way of exercising power elsewhere. To sustain continuity, to uphold ideals and values, to feed whatever one is responsible for so that it flourishes, sometimes at the cost of your own lessening, is not to idealize motherhood but to recognize an archetypal model of power that rarely finds its way into the teaching texts of management with their focus on assertiveness skills, confrontation with insubordination and image projection.

Sustaining has various corollaries: conserving, sharing, allowing. They empower others rather than delegate to others. These corollaries belie the inferior passive idea of matter that we discussed earlier and which informs our hyperenergetic attitudes of productivity and performance. Unlike that passive idea which traditionally says matter must be moved by exertion of superior force (which in practice means the force of a superior in the chain of command), the worldview of sustaining holds that there is an innate potential in each person, in each task, in each creature, animate and inanimate. This potential is not inert; it is, as the Marxists would say, in chains.

The soul in chains or imprisoned belongs to the repertoire of Western philosophical images that go back a long way. Before modern science, the philosophy of nature insisted that there were sparks of fire or soul trapped inside all things. These sparks could be released by various arts, especially alchemy. The idea of an enlivening image trapped inside a dumb block of material informs the arts as far back as Pygmalion, the sculptor, whose statue had life in it, and again, with Michelangelo, whose chisel released the inherent image in the marble, not merely imposing his own image upon the marble.

The alchemist conceived his art to be one of operating with natural forces in such a way as to release the innate potentials locked up and waiting for articulation. The symbol of this transformation from dumb and depressed inaction to maximum fulfillment of potential was gold. All things, if properly tended, could become gold. This alchemical analogy remains viable today for thinking about the application of power as an artful encouraging and releasing of the powers innate in others, maximizing through discretion, rather than direction.

Parallel with the natural philosophy of alchemy and strongly influencing it are ideas of Jewish mysticism. I refer to the Cabalistic idea of *tsim tsum,* or retreat, withdrawal. The Cabalistic argument follows this line of reasoning: Since God is everywhere, "the existence of the universe is made possible by a process of shrinking in

God."* To create, to produce, room must be made for the things of this world. God, so omnipresent, so omnipotent, crowds out all other kinds of existence. So he must pull back for the creation to come into being. Only by withdrawal does God allow the world. The ruling principle at the top must not be omnipresent (being everywhere) and omniscient (knowing everything). Productivity happens by God's getting out of the way. He ignores; becomes an ignorant God; rules by benign neglect. He puts himself in exile. This is hardly the manager who is always learning and increasing his abilities. We have come a long way from subordination.

We can imagine *tsim tsum* happening on a daily human level, where retreat may not feel quite so "divine." It may simply occur as feelings of incapacity, impotence and exile. The sense of being out of touch, not quite in control. If, however, we place these moments against the background of *tsim tsum,* or creation via retreat, these disempowering experiences may be imagined less as weakness than as times requiring an epic strength, very like a God, constricting one's dominion by intelligent self-restraint. Abandoned is that entire fantasy of managing the whole show; abandoned are plans of efficient centralization and supervisory control. Instead, one gives up the reins, the reports, the responsibility in order to allow the potentials in an organization to emerge from their hiding places. The paral-

---

* Gershom Scholem, *Major Trends in Jewish Mysticism* (London: Thames & Hudson, 1955), p. 260.

lel with the arts is rather evident. For what the actor tries to achieve onstage is to "get out of the way" so that the character he or she is portraying can come fully out. So, too, the writer and the painter; they have to get out of the way of the flow of the work onto the paper and the canvas. Parallels with the organization of individual personality need hardly be mentioned. We have to "get out of the way" so that our families can breathe, so our dreams can stay close by in the morning. How far can we go in "not-knowing," in the simple admission of ignorance? It feels like an abdication of all our powers. Biographers of the great sometimes use the term "creative breakdown" for such periods of *tsim tsum* in a human life.

These subtle ideas of power, or ideas of subtle power, that feminism, the arts and mysticism rely upon still do not exhaust the range of our theme. For there are powers beyond whatever we try to formulate. We reach them with gestures and rites. They seem remote from business, government and even psychology. Some do happen in the mind, like dreams that force realities on us that we would not acknowledge; like insights that shock our lives into new patterns. Other powers come through the eyes like the sudden *coup de foudre* of a love affair. Yet others propitiate with prayer or with candles and little stones on private altars at home after a strange coincidence or a bad day. Then there are the animistic powers that inhabit the environment and that the late twentieth century is redis-covering in two ways, the first ecology, the second toxicology. The first says human agency depends on the power of the biosphere to which human existence is subordinated. The second says unsuspected powers reside in the soil and water, the food and the air, the furniture and the walls and the high-tech machines we work with. These can cause disease and death. Ideas of power that start with human agency capitulate before this return of animism. It is the powers out there in places, in things and in minds that now require attention and call for more refined imaginations of power altogether.

Intimations of the subtleties of power return us to an aboriginal feeling of ritual. The brilliant African teacher Malidoma Some writes about agency:

> . . . *no one can accomplish anything who is not in alignment with the Gods or with a God. . . . It does not take much time to send a little invocation at the start and at the end of the day. . . . By ritually putting what we do in the hands of the Gods, we make it possible for things to be done better because more than we are involved in its getting done.* *

Leadership, authority, ambition that moves only in accord with its own vision runs extra risk—the risk of offending powers it does not see. "Because more than we are involved," as Malidoma Some says. Anyone in power must keep one foot in each world, responding to each according to its claims. The instinct on which leadership depends is quite close to intuition, that nose for what's in

---

* *Ritual: Power, Healing and Community* (Portland, OR: Swan & Raven, 1993).

the air. A person in power addresses and is addressed by the subtle forces in the air and acts as a collective trouble-shooter of the troubling spirits, feels upset by them and vulnerable to them. This openness, this capacity to be influenced, and to resist as well, places those in power in communal service to the growth and maintenance of an organization. The subtle powers which you recognize locate you both as an avant-garde and as a confluence of various forces. You are like the individual seed of a communal spirit, giving voice to a more differentiated and comprehensive will.

Subtle kinds of power have been appearing all through this book. Yet the power of conventional definitions continues to subordinate our thinking to such old and familiar notions as: power is basically a subordinating force; agency requires exertion; to have power one must first train the will. We have instead been suggesting, and will now follow up more fully in the next Part, that power does not lie in the hands of human agents only, does not necessitate domination of the Other, and certainly does not exclude emanations of power coming from the simple activities of daily life. Good service, well-maintained structures, the offices we sit in, the language written to us in reports and spoken by us at meetings—these, too, are kinds of power, exerting agency and leading our actions in definite directions. Power emanates from ideas such as efficiency and growth which can grant authority to programs of purism and fear. For by now we have seen the subtle power of ideas that can control, influence or tyrannize how we think and feel about what we do. In short, we have come to recognize the subtleties of power residing in the ideas of power.

3

MYTHS OF POWER—
POWER OF MYTHS

This Part tries another approach to power. If Part Two differentiated typical ideas associated with power, this Part tries to show more directly the power of myths on ideas. Part Two led to the realization that a power drive has many faces and that while one person's perception of power may be prestige, for another it may be authority and influence. Now we will go beyond typical ideas and personal styles as we move from a typology to an archetypology.

Here I am positing patterns of power in the imagination, patterns prior to ideas and revealed in the ideas. These are *archai,* the Greek term for root principles, the basic metaphors on which all things rest and which give consistently typical forms and styles of expression to the way we think, feel and talk. Figures from myths best show these patterns and so figures from myths have become, especially in recent years again, a kind of shorthand taxonomy for classifying patterns of behavior and styles of personality along definite lines. These grids are more like contour maps of the terrain of imagination allowing the mind to read itself imaginatively; whereas explanations are more like bulldozers that flatten the terrain into plain thinking useful for erecting conceptual constructs.

Call these engraved lines archetypes, call them mythical grids, call them imaginal persons or ideational forms, whatever they be named they are to be distinguished from the categories that philosophers like Aristotle and Kant hold to be basic mental structures, abstract categories like space and time, motion and number. Mythical grids are figurative, personified. They are found most easily in the arts (drama, painting, sculpture, poetry, writing styles). Remnants of this practice still adorn public buildings as Goddesses of Justice, of Reason and of Liberty. Once upon a time in Rome—and the Romans knew a thing or two about power—there were statues, shrines and offerings honoring all kinds of powers influencing personal relationships, the conduct of the state and attitudes of the mind. These shrines honoring mythical powers were common in ancient Greece, too. "To mention Athens alone, we find altars and sanctuaries of Victory, Fortune, Friendship, Modesty, Mercy, Peace, and many more." Ugliness, Insolence and Violence were also recognized. These were real powers to be attended to and not "mere figments of the imagination."*

As Gods and Goddesses, these all-powerful structures were thought to determine and qualify major areas of human and cosmic existence. For instance, the Greek and

---

* R. Hinks, *Myth and Allegory in Ancient Art* (London: Warburg Institute, 1939), p. 109.

Roman Ares/Mars, God of fury and battle rage and protector of the city, had a host of places, days and events that "belonged" to him, like the war horse, the spear and the metal iron. He was shielded and defended and little could penetrate his hard-hat helmet. The symbolic ramifications of this virile, red-faced, hirsute god extended his realm to cover countless aspects of daily life: hot foods (peppers, radishes); red stones and flowers; acute illnesses (fevers, rashes); tempos and keys of music, staccato rhythms and galloping beats of poetry; herbal remedies, lore of character, animals like the hawk and woodpecker, geographies that were hot and dry, and a rhetorical style of language that is exhortative, rapid, apodictic. Anything one encountered in people, in nature, in fate, in the sensate world of things "belonged" to one or another mythical figure. The world was an open book and could be read according to the mythical grids of the imagination.

And still today. From the bombs on Baghdad, the brouhahas of basketball, to the battles of fists and blood, Mars still explodes into our living rooms from the bright altars of our TV screens. Car ads (often red), car chases, car races, car wrecks, car crashes in towers of fire. Scenes of catastrophes and accidents—it is as if the entire watching audience were on 911 emergency call. Mars governs not only the content and the images but especially the speed of their delivery: the ellipses that skip the details of a message in order to "get it across" in a flash, the cuts and switches and startling juxtapositions of editing, the rapid fire one-liners, loud applause, hyped-up volume of music breaks and the fast talk all day, all night—disc jockey as man from Mars. Watch the zip-bam-pow cartoons on Saturday mornings; Mars selling candy and toys; TV as mini–boot camp for five-year-olds. Mars loves the manic style that brooks no interruptions and roars forward at breakneck speed while we viewers accommodate, surfing through the channels or viewing two at once by means of split screens and pip windows.

This mythic sense of the patterns operating in the daily world held sway for centuries and was fundamental to the Renaissance. As a mode of understanding, mythical figures seem to be coming back from their long exile in decorative artistic conceits, pop astrology and herbal lore, coming back in some strength not only in the hands of scholarly psychological thinkers like David L. Miller,* Thomas Moore† and Ginette Paris,‡ but also, surprisingly, in Charles Handy's *Gods of Management*.** Handy describes four distinct philosophies and practices of management, each with the name of a Greek mythical figure: Zeus, Apollo, Athene, Dionysos. These are each different cultures within which management operates. Handy writes:

---

* David L. Miller, *The New Polytheism* (Dallas: Spring Publications, 1981).

† Thomas Moore, "Artemis and the Puer," in *Puer Papers,* J. Hillman, ed. (Dallas: Spring Publications, 1979).

‡ Ginette Paris, *Pagan Meditations* (Dallas: Spring Publications, 1986).

** London: Pan Books, 1985. Cf. also James Ogilvy, *Many Dimensional Man* (New York: Oxford University Press, 1977), for an even earlier study employing the classical Gods as structural metaphors.

Each culture, it will become clear, or each god, works on quite different assumptions about the basis of power and influence, about what motivates people, how they think and learn, how things can be changed. These assumptions result in quite different styles of management, structures, procedures and reward systems . . . Different cultures and gods are needed for different tasks. (P. 11.)

The four configurations which Handy elaborates do not cover the whole range of the mythic grid. Of the many others, the heroic style is the easiest to discern. Look at the ads for any "Successful Management" seminar. What do they emphasize? Victory. Achievement. Assertiveness skills. Power thoughts. Peak performance. How to be and stay up. How to be tough on yourself. How to take charge and drive forward. Look, too, at the advice, the rhetoric and the anecdotes spoken by and about the winners: The chairman and CEO of the Home Depot is said to have told this story at a business conference:

Every morning in Africa a gazelle wakes up: It knows it must run faster than the fastest lion or it will be killed.

Every morning the lion wakes up: It knows it must outrun the slowest gazelle or it will starve to death.

It doesn't matter whether you are a lion or a gazelle: When the sun comes up, you'd better be running.

Several times in the previous pages we have referred to heroism because heroes like Hercules are particularly relevant for the patterns governing our ideas of power. The hero not only enlarges the kingdom by overcoming opponents and taking over their realms, not only meets all challengers as adversaries, not only is declared to be stronger, quicker and smarter than all others in a life dedicated to endless competition, the hero like Hercules comes onto the stage as a *soter*, or savior, who initiates a rescue operation to keep an institution from going under.

Handy and the other authors I am mentioning do not judge these patterns in terms of better or worse, as if a Zeusian style of hierarchial supervision were right while the loose and wandering individuality of Handy's Dionysian mode were wrong.* Or to use another pair: as if Apollonian clear order and detached formality were correct and Hermes' tricky and swift decision making was ill considered, hasty and irresponsible. Ginette Paris writes (contrasting Apollo and Aphrodite): "Each of them is necessary to civilization [or management], and a polytheistic mentality should help us to recognize both, without seeking to pit one against the other." (Op. cit., p. 17.) Thomas Moore extends the polytheistic principle further, declaring: ". . . in genuine polytheism conflict can never be reduced to simple dualism, dialectic or two-horned dilemma. A polytheistic perspective always opens out onto increased complexity and additional possibilities." (Op. cit., p. 199.) These contemporary writers follow an ancient caution, from the Greek dramatist Euripides: "Each

---

* On the Dionysian style, see also Mia Nijsmans, "A Dionysian Way to Organizational Effectiveness," in *Psyche at Work*, Murray Stein and John Hollwitz, eds. (Wilmette, IL: Chiron Publications, 1992), pp. 136–55.

God makes a claim on us which we may pay only in the God's coin—this is an inescapable fact."

To imagine a choice among the figures already catches us in adversarial thinking, pitting one pattern against another and setting off a war—or a lawsuit—among the Gods. The task is less one of choosing among the styles than of appreciating diversity. Each situation that management must face will have a different configuration and will make its own peculiar demands which can be settled only in the coin of the mythical figure who shapes the situation at its source. Managerial skill becomes psychological perception, which in turn becomes mythological reflection—that is, a mythic sensibility regarding the roots of trouble. What "coin" is now called for? "Who" is now determining events? Which myth is now at work? Leadership entails learning the patterns, learning the ways of the Gods, so that one does not fall prey to the monotheistic simplification of "one size fits all." As Handy says: "Differences, then, are necessary and good for organizational health. Monotheism, the pursuit of a single god, must be wrong for most organizations." (Op. cit., p. 39.)

How then do we recognize which pattern is dominating an issue. Three rules of thumb can help. First, watch your language. Second, feel your mood. Third, sense how the world responds. All three rules ask for an awareness that problems and decisions have an archetypal context which affects the rhetoric of your thinking, the inwardness of your feeling and the effects you have on others. The archetypal context is like a field that holds you, the problem or decision, and the world together in a common story from which there is no escape and which the Greeks called the plot or myth that governs fate. Issues and situations can be analyzed not only personally in terms of the people involved and systemically in terms of the organization but also archetypally in the deep patterns presented most universally by myths.

Perhaps the clearest way of discerning myths in our ideas is to turn to futurology, the field of scientific models of prediction. These models show a set of familiar configurations appearing again and again. Futurology is governed by present models of thought, yes; also by past experience, yes; and also by timeless *archai* or basic mythical grids. When the human mind works with the unknown—and the future is certainly the unknown—it must invent and imagine. These imaginings about unknowables—such as outer space and farther planets, the interior subjectivity of animals, infants and remote tribes, the origins of life and dispositions after life—are subject to the powers that structure imagination into rather definite repetitive patterns which are projected into the dark field we are exploring and which we claim to see in the evidence we are gathering. What we are seeing is partly skewed by the imagination. When we predict, we project. In fact, future studies are often called "projections." The projection-making factor is in the subjective mind as much as it is in the objective data, and since the deepest structures of the mind are probably archetypal patterns, appearing so regularly and universally in art and thought, ritual and behavior, dreams and madness, we can expect them to display themselves as well in projections about the future. Let's review a few of these familiar fantasies:

1. Cyclical Return of history to patterns we know from the past: ethnic strife and genocide; the Balkanization of Europe; Giant Germany; Greater East Asia Co-Prosperity Sphere as the Japanese in the 1930s and 1940s called the Pacific Rim economy; Yellow Peril; slave revolt; taxpayer revolt; American isolationism; Prohibition ("just say no"); puritanism and censorship; robber barons and cartels (now called multinational corporations enjoying free trade); colonialism (peacekeeping forces by the Western coalition); nature taking care of itself (reseeding after forest fires) through benign neglect; self-regeneration of oceans; recycling and transformation; boundless energy sources. The Great *Ricorso* (Vico), *Ewige Wiederkehr* (Nietzsche). Whatever will happen will be like what has already happened.

2. Gloom and Doom. Stagflation. Zero growth. Permanent high-level unemployment. The same-size pie with ever more demand for larger slices; shrinking resources; scarcities; aging population consuming the earnings of the younger. Fewer healthy babies and more sick mothers and hungry children; more liminals and marginals (genetic mutants, cripples, dyslexics, illiterates, addicts, homeless, jobless, etc.). Racial and ethnic violence. Extinctions of species. Either a submissive and indolent proletariat or a rebellious one. Stricter law enforcement modeled on Latin American quasi-legal methods of the 1970s and 1980s; the Latinization of North America through demography and economics, with the elite in protected compounds, drug lords and gangs ruling warring fiefs, the destitute in shantytowns, and the decline of the middle class. Increased prison populations and armed guards in schools. Corruption of governments. And, over all, the pall of nuclear winter and/or global warming.

3. Hopeful Greening. A New Age of Aquarius. Global village, self-determination of ethnic cohesive societies like Slovakia and Slovenia. New conflict-resolution models. Billions of trees reforested like a thousand points of light; biotechnology for "cleaning up" after environmental disasters. Racial and gender equality. Community care, hospices, day-care centers, parental leave, integrated schools, rebirth of the arts with spiritual and social purpose. Peace dividends. Permissive suicide, permissive sexual affiliations. All the walls tumbling down. Legalized prostitution, legalized marijuana. Creative education. Universal access for the impaired and deprived. Health care and wealth share.

4. Apocalyptic Catastrophe. Nuclear mistakes like Three Mile Island and Chernobyl. Irreversible viral and genetic mutations. Insoluble toxic waste problem leading to cancers and epidemic death of biosystems. Earthquakes. Volcanoes like Mount St. Helens. Jihad, Kahane, Christian Righteousness as rebirth of Nazism. Sahel famines. Rwanda, Somalia, Haiti, Timor, Cambodia. New plagues like AIDS. Suffocation in industrial exhaust. Nuclear terrorism. Ozone depletion—drowning, poisoning and burning of populations through ecological calamities. Epidemic immune-system breakdown. Radical drop in sperm counts. Everyone carrying arms; breakdown of government; dysfunctional cities; kidnapping; carjacking; guerrillas, thugs, yakuza and warlords; Mafia rule. Salvation from outer space.

5. Well-Managed Rationalism. Economic integration of all Europe, North America. New trade accords and ecospheres of rational production, distribution and consumption. Decline and control of weapons production. Ever improved means of transportation and communication; systems design (strategies) for finance and technology to resolve food, population, climate, energy and resource crises. Task forces, SWAT teams, think tanks. Human engineering; increasing longevity; genetic innovation; immunology advances; practical use of outer space. Prozac correctness. Optimistic expectations based on complex statistical data analyses. Ecumenical religious tolerance. Widening integration of women, "minorities," the "disabled" in the society. New needs for services creating new jobs. Social philosophy rather than only market economics determining goals: education, health care, quality of life instead of consumption, production and expansion. Reform of media to reflect social agenda.

These five examples do not exhaust the range of scenarios. Moreover, there are variations and corollaries of each that would refine these projections into the future. Nonetheless, the five examples make my point clearer: there are grids along which the future is projected. Scenarios suggest authors and directors behind the scenes (within the imagination) who guide the designs and shape the language which futurologists seem to "discover" in their empirical evidence. We cannot think at all without basic assumptions, and these assumptions, as *archai,* are probably given with the imagining mind.

If we place the five examples on mythical grids, we might find that behind each is a director, an archetypal direction of thought that gathers the evidence it needs and draws the conclusions it projects according to its view of the world.

1. Cyclical Return suggests the Great Mother of decline, death and renewal. Seasons of climate, phases of the moon, ebb and flow of the tides govern all things. All things repeat, and all things get worse before they get better. The business cycle is an unchanging law, as are the fluctuations of Wall Street: whatever goes up must come down, and vice versa. It is not so much the content of prediction that reflects this particular archetypal perspective as the emphasis on comparisons with former patterns and their inevitable repetition. The Gaia hypothesis of the planet as a living organism is only one of her present manifestations.

2. Gloom and Doom. Old Saturn, lord of outcasts, failures, cripples; exact measurements and rigid sciences like mathematics, founder of the mint and keeper of the purse; eater of his own children, ruler of winter and woe and obdurate endurance. Mr. Scrooge.

3. Hopeful Greening. Perhaps the eternal youth (*puer eternus* of Roman imagery), the adolescent vision of change for the better, far horizons, wings of desire, the elevation of beauty, the quick solution. Peter Pan.

4. Apocalyptic Catastrophe. This is *the* myth of our civilization, because the New Testament ends with the Book of Revelations and the complete annihilation of all things in holocaustal fire in preparation for the Second Coming of Christ. Catastrophe theory offers an abbreviated formulation of this myth that is always lurking in the unconscious death wish of a Christian civilization.

5. Well-Managed Rationalism. Perhaps this reflects no God at all, but the eighteenth-century's Goddess of Reason. Or we can detect in it the well-knitted integrational counsel of Athene/Minerva and the optimism of her father, jovial Zeus/Jupiter, whose self-sufficiency and faith in the power of wit to overcome adversity maintains his Olympian grandiosity.

———

Other directors could give the directions I sketched another slant. Archetypal thinking doesn't necessitate one-
to-one equations, because this thinking is rooted in a polytheistic imagination in which the powers of ideas are
interlinked and mutually influenced. There is no one sure
truth, one sure identity, one sure explanation. The value of
archetypal thinking is not so much to give sure identifica-
tions to problems. Rather, it aims to open the mind to
psychological reflection on the mind's stances and projects.
When I talk about the future and show my charts and
graphs, which mythical figure is influencing what I predict?
Not merely *what* am I seeing, but *who* is seeing? Who is
shaping the evidence and drawing the conclusions? According to which perspective and along which mythical grid?
The moment I can step back from my own presentation
and ask "who?" I am examining my own subjectivity for
the imaginational factors that more or less unconsciously
steer my selection of data, priority of values and specific
conclusions.

Precisely this stepping back is the moral of the archetypal approach to ideas. It claims that to be ever more
objective, we need to be ever more subjectively alert to
the dominants of imagination that let us, or make us, see
and say things in certain well-defined ways. If we don't
know who is at work in an idea, we more easily get caught
by its power. We become identified with that idea, defend
it, fight for it, and soon we have become ideational funda-
mentalists, believing firmly in an idea because it "really is

right." The clashes between people in companies and marriages are the wars of the Gods whose oversize Olympian power gives ideas such conviction. The feeling of certitude must come from somewhere below or beyond the usual ego, so it is the identification with the power within an idea that gives to its promulgator the feeling of certainty.

Myths can account for even that feeling of certainty. It, too, comes from the Gods, says the story of Cassandra. Apollo wanted her and gave her the gift of prophetic insight by wetting her lips with his tongue. But she then refused his desire and so he gave her as well the curse that no one would believe what she saw so certainly. Although she could surely foretell what was to come, her warnings fell on unheeding ears. She could tell only the truth and was considered, by her fellow Trojans, insane.

The feeling of certainty depends neither on acceptance by others nor on confirmation by events. It comes altogether from elsewhere, as it came to Cassandra from Apollo. That is its truth, and its tragedy, and its potential for paranoid insanity. Do you see how myths complicate matters—causing the mind to be ever more doubting, subtle and sophisticated even in regard to certainty itself?

In addition to the five visions of the future summarily sketched above, we need to look at a mythical figure so dominant in our present activities that his power seems to grow by leaps and bounds—an appropriate metaphor for

Hermes/Mercury, the Greek and Roman God of magic wand, flying thoughts and winged feet.

The pile of stones that go back to prehistoric times and that stood symbolically for him mark the edge, the fringe, the limits. He set the boundaries—and overcame them, too, by making passages between near and far, familiar and foreign, this world and other worlds above and below. So Hermes/Mercury is the God of messages, communication, commercial exchange, marketplace. He is the God of everyone on the road between here and there, unsettled, volatile. And he is the God of language, interpreter of invisibilities, audacious liar, artful craftsman and easygoing thief with a special relation to the Underworld. His arrival is instantaneous, a flash of inspiration; innovative, cunning, delicate in depictions yet also phallic and seminal. As lord of gates, doors and the open road, he gives access and spins the miracles of networking.

Do we not live in a world dominated by his kind of power? Does not anyone in the market—and not only Boesky, Milken, Keating and Jett—owe a coin to Hermes/Mercury? He may be imagined in other borderline areas as well. High-energy physics of invisible hadrons, particle accelerators, superconductivity of frictionless transmission and the principle of complementarity appear to be governed by Hermes rather than by the stable rules and classical laws of Apollo, while the relation to the natural world calls less on Artemisian reverence and piety for its protection than on innovative mercurial cunning that can shift genes and outwit germs, invent sexual lures and hybrid seeds. Even the strategic planning of war, classically a province of Athene, and the martial battlefield fury depend now altogether on electronic sophistication and instant communication (and night vision—Hermes could make stealthy passages in darkness).

Although I live four miles from the nearest news-stand, gas station and convenience store, messages of every sort enter my home, even while I sleep. Fax, modem, cable, answering machine, call waiting, satellite dish, car phone, Lexis/Nexus, Internet, E-mail and a time-set VCR. I am plugged into the whole wide world and can enjoy media shopping, media investing, media counseling and media sex. Access unlimited. My telephone and fax bills show communications each month with twenty states and a dozen different countries. Yet I am merely one relatively retired, quietly industrious, rural citizen. My friends and professional advisers, my students and family members are spread widely. Yet I reach out and touch someone every day, invisibly, immediately, electronically. This is Hermes/Mercury. My actions are rituals that give recognition to his power and my electronic service station establishes his shrine at which I kneel on my backless stool.

Besides these facilities, I engage in other Hermetic/Mercurial activities. My mind continually interprets the world, watching for signs and portents, searching out symbolic meanings, engaged in hermeneutics. I belong to the time of spin doctors and virtual realities which can fix up facts, twist and trick words and images so that appearance and reality, memory and imagination, illustration and illusion can no longer be distinguished. I have learned the initiate's secret language of software, database, peripherals, floppy disks, gadgets, acronyms and abbreviations which open windows, allowing exchange with anyone, anywhere, or with no one definite and particular. Frankly phallic Hermes sends scurrilous anonymous messages through the Internet, and shady adolescent hackers steal my thoughts and violate my privacy.

Whether or not this is the future, it is the present and we need to recognize that the hypertrophy of communication can become a disease endemic to the electronic culture. C. G. Jung wrote that "the Gods have become diseases." They affect us through our systems, our behavior, the unknown mysteries that afflict our lives. This hypertrophy of communication is the disease wrought by Hermes/ Mercury. The potential for disease lies in any God; any grid can become an obsessional rut when a single vision is lived one-sidedly and monotheistically adored above all others.

In the Greek world Hermes was frequently paired with Hestia,* Goddess of the interior hearth, the one first

---

* On the characteristics of Hermes and Hestia, see William G. Doty, "Hermes' Heteronymous Appellations," *Facing the Gods,* J. Hillman, ed. (Dallas: Spring Publications, 1980); Barbara Kirksey, "Hestia—A Background of Psychological

honored in all ceremonies. Her Roman priestesses were keepers of the salt that gives savor to the common everyday and catches flying birds by the tail; preservation, unchanging. She was figured only by a round central stone, a place of fire. Hestia, the self-contained virgin; Hermes, invisibly penetrating boundaries, transgressing limits. She was the ever present intimate inside, as he was the outside; she, stillness, he, all motion; she, concentrated focus (*focus*, Latin for hearth), he, multiple participation on the roads everywhere.

Just as we can witness Hermes's power running wild in the circuits of our psychological wiring, we can discover the complementary power of Hestia inspiring, first, the idea of therapy and, second, the idea of servant leadership.

Hundreds of thousands, if not millions, of those engaged in the mercurial life of markets, communication, sales, travel and dissemination of the word are at the same time protecting and conserving their interior fires with the Hestian quiet of therapy. As Goddess of the inner flame that keeps a home and a city, and each person, alive, she calls those most captivated by the wings of Mercury to remember the other half of the pair by going "into" and staying "in" therapy for the sake of maintaining a focus,

Focussing," in ibid.; Paola Pignatelli, "The Dialectics of Urban Architecture—Hestia and Hermes," *Spring: A Journal of Archetype and Culture* (Dallas: Spring Publications, 1985); Wolfgang Fauth, "Hermes," *Spring,* idem, 1988; Stephanie Demetrakopoulos, "Hestia, Goddess of the Hearth," *Spring,* idem, 1979.

often called "centering," in the busy midst of a mercurial life. Hestia reminds Hermes that alone he has no focus to his vision; it's all peripheral.

Servant leadership, a theory and practice invented by Robert Greenleaf (formerly director of management research at AT&T), reinstates service as a primary form of power most suitable for a coming century. Laying emphasis on listening, acceptance and empathy, servant leadership functions in an introverted manner by means of interior connections, soul to soul. Although the language and the idea clearly reflect the suffering servant figures of Isaiah and Jesus, it is the focus of deep intimate attention that Hestia offers to this school of leadership, rather than the elevation of suffering in the Christian model. Hestia's service is not a suffering. She makes life immediately felt, not instantaneous like Hermes, but immediate as in right here, close, intense, concrete as salt, direct as fire, this moment, a steady dwelling on the matter at hand.

Whereas "I," this Everyman of the future, do not dwell. My home is not my castle; it is my office, and a tax write-off. My house is protected with automatic timers that turn on the radio, CD player, TV (which records shows while "I" is on another coast). Outside lights go on and off with sensitizers to keep the building burglarproof (fantasies of Hermes the thief). No one need be home. The house runs by itself; the hearth is a thermostat. To be is to be plugged in, the computer never down; all systems running on Hermes's swift feet.

Since my friends are on the phone and on the fax, I can ignore my neighbor's comings and goings. I'm doubled up with call waiting. My news is of Panama, Namibia, Romania—not the local board of education, the planning and zoning commission, the community obituaries. My charities are major: the homeless in New York, the refugees in Miami, the AIDS cases in San Francisco, not the jobless down the road who live on food stamps and meager pensions. I don't even know who they are. Greenpeace for whales in the Arctic—but what about the local songbirds? Cable has such great shows, who needs a local hangout? "I" lives everywhere but here.

Hermes is not wrong, nor is Hestia right. Nor am I pleading for moderation and balance between them. Improving the mix, a little more of one and a bit less of the other. My point is not so much moral and practical as psychological, and it is about power.

When we looked at the kinds of power in Part Two, we differentiated styles and meanings. They seemed merely a series of shadings of words giving different emphasis. These styles also seemed available to reason. Surely, a person can separate tyranny and domination from authority and influence. In that first look, power seemed something we could bring into rational control.

This second look shows power of another kind, or at a different level. This is a power that runs our lives by dominating our ideas about our lives. This perspective says that we behave according to archetypal ideas along the lines of mythical grids. This kind of power is out of our hands and places us in the hands of the Gods and Goddesses who work within the psyche through complexes, symptoms, traits, instincts and fantasies.

One of the greatest of the Greek dramatists, Euripides, said that "all things are full of Gods." To me this means the dog at my feet, the tree in my yard, the stones that hold up my house—and also the bus that takes me to work and the workstation where I sit. If "all things are full of Gods," then we humans, too, our inner workings, our very ideas, are full of Gods. We, too, are subject to myths even if the main God in our personal pantheon, whom we consciously bear witness to at the beginning of most sentences we speak, is the capitalized ego, "I." "I" doesn't believe myths are real, so they cannot have power. "I" has become that monocentric God who creates what is real by declaring it is real, thereby shaping the world according to his own theology.

If the thesis of mythical grids has some validity, then the declarations of independence made by "I" must be read as protests. "I" fears sharing power with these others, which, by denying, he may make disappear but which nevertheless pull his strings from behind the scenes. To repeat the poet Auden again: "We are lived by powers we pretend to understand."

My point here is psychological and not at all religious in the usual sense of belief. "I" is not being asked to believe. A psychological sense of powers who fill our minds and actions in the cellars and at the edges of "I's" kingdom does not require prayer, priest or writ, does not ask for witness or testimony, does not load guilt. A psychological sense of them is merely an awareness, almost primitive and naive, that though the will be bankrupt and the heart in despair, you can never be all alone, never powerless. Something has you always in mind.

Closing: On Power and Powers

A word or two before we part: All through these pages there has been a hidden agenda, a polytheistic worldview. It claims that the most basic powers of imagination are the invisible myths which lay out our thoughts and actions in line with universal patterns. In our culture these dominant powers have Greek and Roman names, and parallels can easily be found in other cultures—Egyptian, Eskimo, Haitian, Polynesian, West African, Native American. Shades of difference, yes; Gods and Goddesses always have local habitations and varieties of names, though often similar faces. For a predominantly Eurocentric culture, the Greek/Roman patterns are the most relevant and most differentiated, and thus the most powerful. By powerful, I mean influential, authoritative, prestigious, controlling and tyrannical. Even if these patterns of imagination that govern our thought and action are utterly patriarchal and therewith condemned as dangerously death-dealing, like a toxic dump of the spent fuel on which civilization has lived for millennia, they are the roots. Inescapable. Multiculturalism cannot jump out of the melting pot that was cast in bronze in Greece centuries ago. So long as this culture is traditionally and officially committed to Indo-European languages and institutions of government and education, of family structures, and modes of thought that define the arts, sciences, religions and human nature, we cannot change our minds, though we may beautifully extend them, revise them and reimagine them.

By exposing these old rooted ideas of power by which we mainly live and still conduct our business, and by adhering to them, rather than junking them as remnants of a defunct patriarchy, we were able to entertain ideas in this book that have been springing up all around the contemporary scenery. Some of them are: less demeaning ideas of maintenance and service, subtle notions of power that do not begin in subordination, kinds of growth which bear more truly on the business of life in this period of history. But the world may not be entering a kinder and gentler new age where happier models drawn from the arts and mysticism replace models of turbines, stress and high-tension lines in our thinking about management, production and generativity. The fearsomeness, the sadism and the clutching grip of the human hand will never ever convert entirely to the palm of soothing and blessing.

The voice which rises from the ashes of Auschwitz (or Treblinka) that represents the culmination of Eurocentric culture says, "The world is ruled by power."* Imme-

---

* Otto Friedrich, *The End of the World* (New York: Coward, McCann & Geoghegan, 1982), p. 294, quoting the poet Tadeusz Borowski: "Concentration-camp

diately the statement is contested by another voice that says the world is ruled by love, and that is why each time power claims dominance we are shocked. We feel in our hearts that the world can't really be so vicious and violent, and that love, which does not show its hand as does power, nonetheless steers all things from within and behind in small invisible ways. Power may parade and bluster and imprison, but love makes values endure. Love conquers all.

These voices that insist upon a contest between love and power are Western, Northern, Christian and romantic. Partly they are reflected in a simplistic division of the Bible into an Old Testament of power and a New Testament of love. What results from this opposition but a loveless power of tyranny and control, and a powerless love that can wish but not will? Love and power are not opponents; it is our ideas that have constructed them so. By moving our ideas we have begun to uncover the concealed benevolence in such formerly loveless notions of power as ambition, exhibitionism, prestige, resistance and even fear. We have also been able to recognize how persuasion, purism, tyranny, control and influence enter into the practice of love, reinforce its agency and give to love such a subordinating power over life.

The resolution of this tiresome contest between

existence . . . taught us that the whole world is really like a concentration camp . . . There is no crime that a man will not commit in order to save himself. The world is ruled by neither justice nor morality, crime is not punished nor virtue rewarded, one is forgotten as quickly as the other. The world is ruled by power."

power and love requires but one simple step, a move from the singular to the plural. Just add an *s*. The world is not one world, power is not a single idea, and love, which comes in thousands of varieties and even more disguises, is a generic commodity, unable to be owned by any single definition.

So, too, business; just add an *s* to profit—profit not only for partners and shareholders. The monotheism of the profit motive can be loosened so that it makes places for other kinds of profitability: profitable for the long-term continuity of life and future generations, profitable to the pleasure and beauty of the common good, profitable to the spirit. The double bottom line of social and ecological responsibility extends profitability only part way. The idea of profit itself needs pluralizing.

Adding the little *s* has been what this book is all about. And so this book has deliberately complicated the one term, "power," differentiating its meanings with the intent of sophisticating our minds. All along I have been suggesting that actions of clean and clear simplicity require a mind aware of complexities. For action to be direct and single, thought must be diverse and plural. Thought is able to contain a plurality of options, a diversity of contrasting implications, and it can foresee the kinds of consequences that ensue from its ideas. When thought is too simple to contain ambiguity, it seeps into action as ambivalence. Thought must do and doubt, both; otherwise action will be

undone by the hesitations of "second thoughts" which confuse its direction and cripple its force.

Myth plays a major role in this sophistication of
thought. During the European Renaissance the ancient
myths were revived and the Gods and Goddesses restored
as dominants of imagination and categories of reflection.
This revival gave to Renaissance thought immense complexity. Single-mindedness was splintered into a pantheon
of possibilities. Meanings proliferated. Yet action during
this same period was spectacularly decisive and enduring.
Scientific experiment, global exploration, financial innovation and artistic accomplishment were carried out boldly,
all the while paradox and subtle innuendo governed
thought.

The lesson I draw from Renaissance subtlety justifies
the mythical excursions and ideational amplifications that
you have patiently absorbed while going through these
pages. All along, by means of myths, word roots and dictionary definitions I have been surreptitiously rewriting
that ubiquitous bumper-sticker slogan of our times, the
one urged by environmentalists: "Think globally; act lo-
cally," translating it into "Think subtly; act simply." To
achieve the subtlety, I have tried to expand all the issues
broached in this book toward the diversity of a polytheistic
vision. Because power is not single, it cannot be mastered
by any single idea. Our own Christian and Jewish traditions
distinguish a variety of powers: in the Hebrew and Greek

texts of the Bible, at least twenty-five different terms—*el, zeroa, chayil, koach, izzuz, dynamis, arche, kratos,* etc., etc.— have been unified by our translations into the single word "power."*

Instead of power, we must speak of powers, and then we will no longer be able to locate them all in a single place, such as the sole agency of the human will. Besides, there are powers in the human, like passionate devotion and the tyranny of an ideology, which the will itself suffers from and surrenders to. And there are powers altogether beyond human agency which other cultures acknowledge by sacrificing a chicken,† by lighting a candle, giving alms, making signs, dances and gestures. These powers outside our agency, according to the greatest phenomenologist of religions, Gerardus van der Leeuw,‡ are the source of whatever we mean by the word "God" and whatever we do when we practice "religion." In this book, however, we did not follow his direction down avenues of priestly, shamanistic and theological powers, nor did we take power along the roads analyzed by George Santayana (in a late work of his old age, *Dominations and Powers*), by Elias Canetti *(Crowds and Power)*, by Norman Cousins *(The Path-*

* Cf. Robert Young, *Analytical Concordance to the Bible* (7th ed.; London: Society for Promotion of Christian Knowledge, n.d.), entry "Power."

† Cf. Luis Manuel Núñez, *Santería* (Dallas: Spring Publications, 1992); Seldon Rodman and Carole Cleaver, *Spirits of the Night: The Vaudun Gods of Haiti* (Dallas: Spring Publications, 1992).

‡ Gerardus van der Leeuw, *Religion in Essence and Manifestation* (2 vols.; New York: Harper Torchbooks, 1963).

ology of Power) or the classic works by Karl Marx, Max Weber and Eric Voegelin.

A third course, more familiar to me, we also did not pursue: the idea of powers that depth psychology has placed in the unconscious psyche—instincts, complexes, drives, memories, emotions. These, too, like the powers of religion and of the state, are beyond the individual will.

Rather than these approaches that would have framed our examination in the stricter fields of religion, politics or psychology, I have tried to show that the powers beyond the human will affect our daily business. We live in their aura constantly. What may have an effect more powerful than heaven above, the intercession of angels and the magic of demons are the ideas that inhabit our minds and go unnoticed in our daily conduct. Of all the little and big forces that subordinate our actions to superior powers it is ideas that hold the most direct and immediate sway. More than the figures of myth, more than the political state, more than the unconscious complexes of emotions, we are subject to ideas through which we filter and by which we form the powers of religion, politics and psychology. Yes, the Holocaust writer was right: the world is ruled by power, the power of ideas.

Nothing dies forever, says myth, even what we judge to be wrong and put behind us as "history." Treblinka, that apogee of despotic power, was there in imagination before Treblinka was built and is still there after Treblinka was leveled. Everything finds its way back into the tent of the mind, if only into the freaky sideshows of pathology. The polytheistic gridworks of myths keep all the rings going at once, providing also the safety nets and stay wires that keep the whole show from falling apart. Once we let go of the obsessive idea of a single center and the idea of order as unity, things can't really fall apart. They simply go on performing their variety acts, each according to its kind —jugglers, clowns, tigers and horses and daredevil leaps on the flying trapeze; round and round, the mind endlessly entertaining, and being entertained by, ideas.

INDEX